Oliver Heath's
home book

Oliver Heath's

home

book

CASSELL
ILLUSTRATED

To my grandfather for the inheritance of his vibrant nature
To my father for endless childhood mornings of enthusiastic DIY
To my mother for the culture that she bought to our home
And to those who have played a part in my design nurture.

First published in Great Britain in 2004 by Cassell Illustrated
A division of Octopus Publishing Group
2–4 Heron Quays, London E14 4JP

This paperback edition published in 2006 by Cassell Illustrated

Distributed in the United States of America by
Sterling Publishing Co., Inc.
387 Park Avenue South, New York,
NY 10016-8810

A CIP record for this book is available from the British Library.

Editor: Robin Douglas-Withers
Design: Carl Hodson
Illustrations: Gavin Reece
Special photography: Sam Bailey
Additional picture research: Lisa Thiel

ISBN-13: 978-1-844034-02-4
ISBN-10: 1-84403-402-X

10 9 8 7 6 5 4 3 2 1

Printed in China

Foreword When I sat down and decided to write this book I was conscious of the fact that these days people are becoming increasingly aware of design and what it can bring to their lives. The way that we design and decorate our homes now says more about us than the clothes we wear. It has in effect become an essential form of self-expression. This is to our benefit as it not only creates a solid foundation for our home lives, but also lets those who visit our homes know who we really are on the inside.

The problem is that while we crave this form of self-expression, knowing the right way to go about it is not always clear. Television programmes and magazines would have us believe that designers just turn up at a house and create a little bit of magic that will have the homeowner crying with tears of joy – or sometimes misery! The reality is that strong design is firmly based in good planning and the two go inextricably together. This planning takes time, needs drawings and requires careful thought if the end product is to be beautiful and within budget. There is a clear thought process that needs to be followed in order for this to be achieved. This process involves 20 per cent practical thinking, 30 per cent soul-searching to discover what it is that you really want, 25 per cent inspiration, 10 per cent financial planning and 30 per cent energy and determination to complete it.

OK, I know that adds up to over 100 per cent – but the best things in life don't come that easy and, when they do arrive, they are amazingly rewarding and something for you to really take pleasure in. How many things in your life can you really say that about?

There is also a sense from the media that we have gone so far down the road of knowing how to do up our homes that we don't need to talk about the basic rules of interior design, that we instinctively know how to carry out complicated design tasks just because we've seen the final result. In my experience this is one of the areas that people really know the least about and find it hard to break down into a clear manageable form.

This book sets out to cover two main issues. Firstly, it aims to let you know the tools of interior design with which you can work. These are the basic building blocks for creating your perfect home and include elements such as your planning process, flooring, lighting, storage and wall finishes. All the options available as well as their benefits and disadvantages are explained.

Secondly, the book shows how you can implement your design in every room of the house by incorporating each of these elements with a little inspiration into your room design. I have consciously tried not to prescribe the type of style that you should opt for – but instead have laid out all the choices in the hope that you will use this information to decide for yourself the look and style that is right for you.

In addition to these two issues, this book contains a mine of other information that will be useful to you, when setting up or adding to your home, such as architectural advice, a section on greener homes, which was written with the help of Friends of the Earth, a list of tools that you might find useful, and a glossary for those more technical terms.

I believe that the home should be an exciting, relaxing, stimulating and comforting place to be, and how you treat your home should reflect how you handle the environment around you when you walk out of your front door. Understanding how you can be more environmentally friendly within the home is something that we all need to do, and it really is easier than you may think.

Your home can be a rewarding place to live and although undergoing change can be difficult and stressful at times, making the decision to create a home that says more about you and that will service your needs in an easier way will make your life more pleasurable and fulfilled.

I hope you enjoy this book and take away from it ideas and processes that will help you to explore what your home can be, and what it can do for you.

Oliver Heath

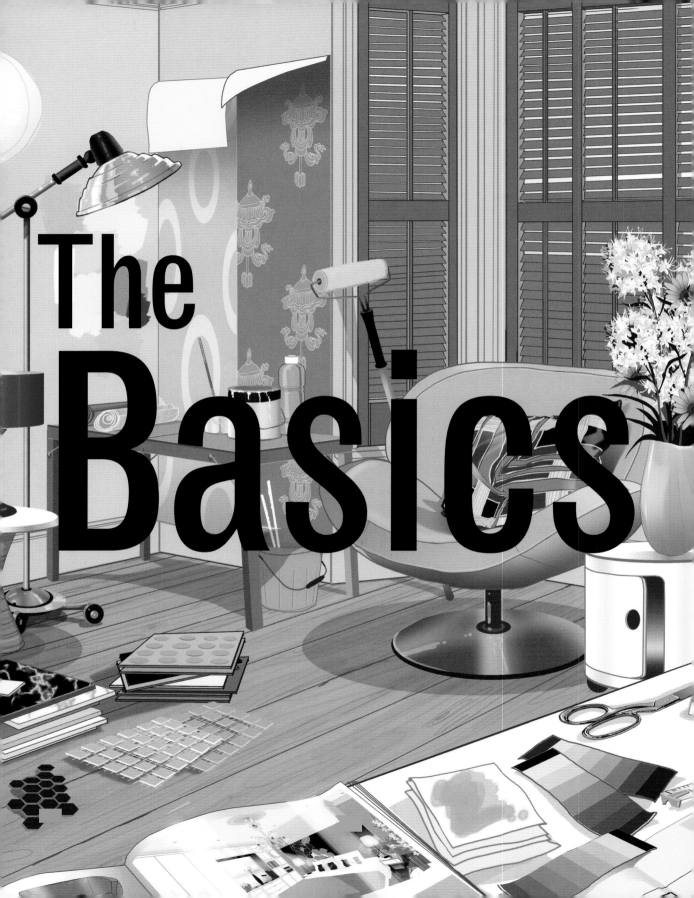

The Basics

So there it is – you push open the door and before you lies an empty characterless space. You look around and wonder just how you are going to turn this blank canvas into the home of your dreams. Sometimes it's the first step that's the hardest to take. I often find sitting down in front of a blank piece of paper quite daunting – it's the expectation and the endless possibilities that make this decision-making process so difficult. This is even more complex if your decisions involve making over an existing space that isn't currently working for you. So just how are you ever going to find the right solution?

Essential and creative planning

Tricks of the trade The key is to break down your decisions into manageable sections that help you plan out your room and narrow down a possible direction for your design. Good design is akin to a juggling act, in which room function, colour, lighting, flooring, wall finishes, furniture, fabrics and budget all need to appear, and trying to make sure they fit together can seem overwhelming. But stay calm... If you follow a relatively simple design process you can consider all the necessary aspects and create something really stunning and practical for yourself and your home.

For me, the early stages of a project are almost as exciting as seeing the final piece come together. It's all about getting to know the parameters of the area, defining its function, understanding the natural light and creating the concept, which can be the most rewarding, creative aspects of interior design. Inevitably, if you have a good idea it can be carried out to suit a variety of different budgets, so have the ideas first and then work out how they will fit together financially.

While this may be the most creative time of the design process it is also the moment when you need to sit down and really focus on all the different aspects that you need to incorporate into the space. At this stage good planning is essential to minimize time delays and expensive mistakes. Despite everything that television programmes and the media would have us believe, good design takes a little time, a lot of thought and plenty of planning.

Where do you begin? To start off the design process ask yourself some basic questions to get your thoughts going in the right direction. These questions are a combination of the practical and the stylistic ideas you will need to consider in order to progress the design through in a balanced way.

Answer these questions and you'll find the mass of ideas will start to narrow down:

► How big is the area? What are the key dimensions that I need to know, both across the floor (known as the plan) and the room's height (known as the section)?

► Are there other elements I need to be aware of – for example, the radiators, the windows, the location of electrical sockets, lights and light switches?

► What design concept do I want to create, what's my big idea?

► What atmosphere do I want to create?

► What colours do I want to use?

► What are the functions of the area, i.e. what activities will I carry out here?

► What will I need to store here?

► What furniture will I need to put into the room?

► What is the natural daylight like?

► What sort of lighting will I need for both daytime and night-time use?

Understanding your space

Knowing the exact size of your space is the essential first step for creating a workable design. It allows you to order furniture that will fit and to buy the right quantities of materials; it stops you wasting money and, if you are clever about it, will give you warning that the expensive luxury king-size waterbed that you have just ordered won't fit along the corridor, let alone through your front door!

Do you get the picture? You must measure your space and, when considering any aspect of the design, you should refer back to these measurements. Don't worry if you've never measured an area before – it doesn't have to be a daunting process and it really can be very straightforward if you are rational about it.

You will need:

▶ A surface to write on, such as a clipboard

▶ A piece of squared or graph paper

▶ A tape measure – 3 or 5 m (10 or 16 ft)

▶ A ruler, pencil and rubber

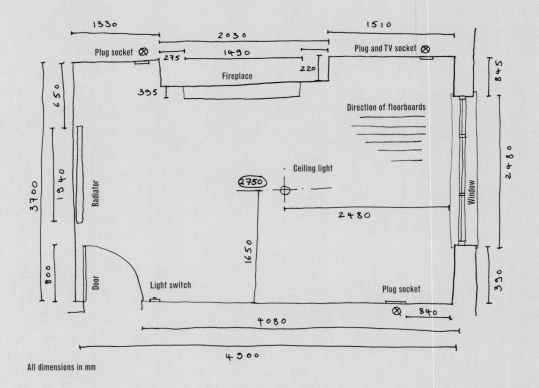

1330   2030   1510

Plug socket ⊗   275   1490   Plug and TV socket ⊗

Fireplace   220

650

845

395

Direction of floorboards

3700

1940

Radiator

Ceiling light

(2750)

2480

Window

2480

800

1650

Door

Light switch

330

Plug socket

⊗   840

4080

4900

All dimensions in mm

Rough plans Start by drawing a rough plan of the room on paper. To do this, imagine that you are looking down on the room from above and draw out the shape of it as accurately as you can, indicating any additional features such as the door (and the area of the arc taken up as it swings open), the windows, radiators and electrical sockets.

Next, take the tape measure and, starting at one corner, work your way methodically around the room, measuring the length of the walls. Write down each measurement next to the corresponding line on your drawing, trying to keep it as neat as you can so that no mistakes are made later on. Once you have

Sketch out a rough outline plan of the room, and add the dimension measurements as neatly as you can.

done this, take overall measurements across the length and width of the room. You should also take a height measurement and indicate it by putting a circle around it.

And now, for a really professional plan, draw the room to scale using the squared paper and a ruler. Allocate squares on the graph paper to represent each actual measurement of your room – for example, two 1 cm (⅓ in) squares per metre – and draw out the shape of the room. Now draw on any key measurements you might need to know, such

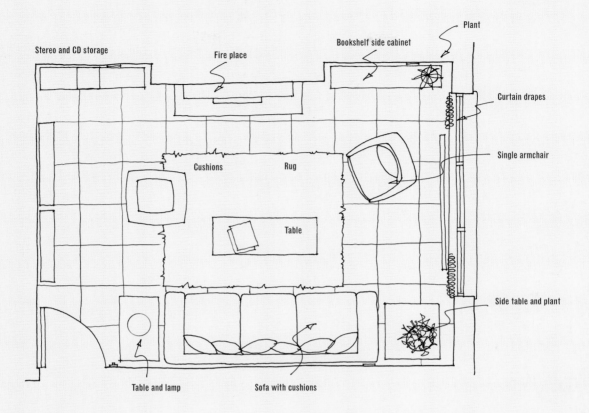

Stereo and CD storage
Fire place
Bookshelf side cabinet
Plant
Curtain drapes
Single armchair
Cushions
Rug
Table
Side table and plant
Table and lamp
Sofa with cushions

as widths and lengths and the door width opening. Take this drawing around with you when making any purchasing or ordering decisions as specific measurements can be difficult to remember.

Furniture to scale Complete the plan by drawing on it to the same scale any essential pieces of furniture that have to be positioned in the room and in the locations you think best. Alternatively, if you are unsure where to position items, draw the pieces of furniture to the same scale on another piece of graph paper then cut them out and play around with the possibilities on your master plan. Some

Draw the plan up to scale on squared paper and add furniture elements to get a sense of the scale of the room.

forward planning here will save you lugging around heavy items once they are in the room.

Try to imagine when you position each piece how the room will be used, how it will look when you walk in through the door, how you will move around the room (don't block pathways) and what the light will be like. Also, do you want to make a focus of any features, make the most of any views from the windows or arrange the furniture around the television? Leave space around the sides of furniture so as not to make the arrangement feel squashed

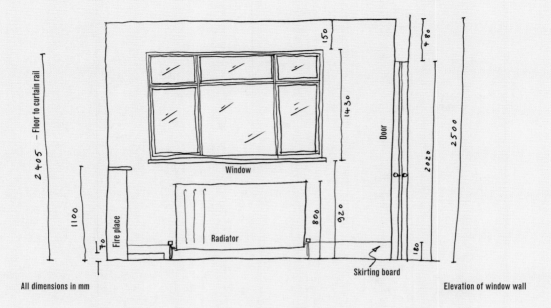

2 405 – Floor to curtain rail

1 100

70

Fire place

Radiator

Window

150

1 430

800

920

Skirting board

Door

640

2 020

480

2 500

180

All dimensions in mm

Elevation of window wall

and allow at least 70 cm (28 in) of 'circulation space' for moving around objects. Considering the layout possibilities is a key part of the design process, so try to stretch your imagination as much as possible and look for unusual combinations. Then assess the suitability of each layout and try to eliminate unworkable solutions.

Vertical heights Don't think of your room only in plan form (looking straight down on it from above); also carry out this measuring and drawing process for each wall so that you understand the vertical heights of elements such as windows, ceilings, work surfaces, shelves, skirting boards and radiators. This allows you to calculate wall surface areas in order to estimate quantities for wallcoverings or even material for curtains. It is also the best

Draw wall elevations to understand the vertical elements of the room.

way to plan specific wall finishes such as murals or even that fantastic stencilling you saw on television last week.

Again, sketch out the shape of the walls onto some paper then transfer the measurements onto graph paper, drawing them to a specific scale. It is very important to try to give a sense of scale to these drawings. A helpful tip is to draw the outline of a standing adult to the same scale to the side of the drawing so you can keep this clearly in your mind.

Put it in perspective My last hot tip for planning out a room is to do a perspective drawing of the area. For those of you who have not picked up a pencil since school, this might strike a note of horror in your hearts. But wait... I wouldn't leave you high and dry like that without a cheatproof method!

The easiest way of creating a realistic perspective drawing is to use a camera and take a series of photos that can be stuck together, then simply sketched over using tracing paper. Turn the camera to take portrait- rather than landscape-orientated pictures, and stand in a corner of the room or by a door. Point the camera to the wall to your left and take a picture, now turn to your right and take another shot, overlapping a little of what was in the first picture, and continue until you get to the wall on your right-hand side. When the photos are printed, line them up next to each other, then stick them together with sticky tape on the rear. You can now trace over the photos with a simple line drawing.

Don't worry if your first drawing is messy and the lines of the furniture are scrappy, just trace over the first drawing to tidy it up. You can now photocopy this lovely neat drawing and use it to try out colour schemes and different fabrics or to draw on pieces of furniture. It's a really great way for getting simple yet realistic drawings of your room.

1

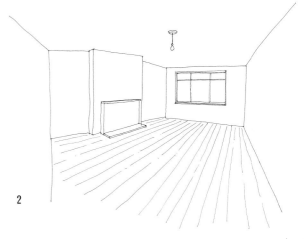

2

3

Create a perspective drawing of the room using collaged photographs, and then trace over them – this will help you to visualise your finished space.

Concepts and ideas

Concepts and ideas Having a strong idea or concept of the way you want your home to look and operate is an essential first step in the creative design process. It's the more fun and imaginative twin to the practical side of measuring up your home and understanding its dimensions. The concept is the point that you will return to again and again when making decisions. If you've got it right it will guide you towards making the right decisions in every aspect of what you want to create... so put your best thinking cap on and work out what it is that you really want from your home.

After years of television make-over shows it's worth remembering that design doesn't have to be an overdressed pantomime fantasy. Creating your room or home can often be a time of self-reflection and honesty about how you live your life, what you want to show, (or hide) and what you want to say about yourself. Getting your home right will allow clearer thoughts and a less cluttered life, letting you get on and do what you want to do.

So how do you get to this perfect concept? It's all about asking the right questions – in terms of practicality, style, culture, experience and lifestyle – and about being honest with the answers. Below are a selection of questions that I always ask people when commencing the design of their homes that can help you in the right direction.

Practicalities

▶ Do my possessions clutter my home and life?

▶ Do I want to make my home feel bigger and more airy, or smaller and cosier?

▶ What practical objects do I need around me? For example, stereo, television, furniture, appliances.

▶ Are there any piles of objects lying around my home that need to be dealt with?

▶ Am I naturally tidy or messy?

Style

▶ What is my style? (Think about what you like to wear or what other sorts of spaces you feel comfortable in or excited by.)

▶ What sort of decorative details do I like? For example, contemporary, minimal, eclectic, ethnic, historical, nature-inspired or retro.

Culture

▶ Are there objects or styles that reflect my background or family history?

▶ Are there objects or styles that reflect my choices in contemporary culture, for example films, music, sports activities, books, fashion?

Experience

▶ Do I have collections of objects that I want to put on show?

▶ Do I have photos or artwork that I would like to display?

▶ What objects that say something about me do I want to have around me?

▶ What do I feel is beautiful?

▶ Have I travelled anywhere that I would like to inspire my home?

Lifestyle

▶ How do I use my home in the daytime?

▶ How do I use my home in the evening?

▶ How do I use my home at weekends?

Answering these questions should help define many of the issues that you need to consider in your home, and from there it is up to you as to which direction to take. You can use your answers to these questions to help you decide upon how you are going to use the basic tools of interior design: colour, lighting, furniture, wall finishes, floor finishes, fabrics, styling, texture and pattern.

Very often, it is the simple ideas that work the best as they are the easiest from which to draw inspiration and to apply to all aspects of interior design. Life is complicated enough as it is, so remember, the simpler you keep your concept, the easier it is to get it right.

Tips for small spaces:

▶ Don't fill the space with too much (or over-sized) furniture; keep it to scale, and give each piece enough space.

▶ Buy furniture that is raised off the floor on legs, so you can see more floor.

▶ Built-in furniture, such as cupboards will make the maximum use of available space.

▶ Paint ceilings, skirting boards and window frames white to keep the room light and fresh.

▶ Use any available floor to ceiling height by putting storage underneath furniture, such as having a raised bed.

▶ Use your walls efficiently with shelving and other storage items to get stuff off the floor.

▶ Use large mirrors to increase the sense of space and to bounce light around the room

▶ Light the otherwise dark corners of a room with small sidelights.

▶ Position furniture such as tables in the middle of rooms to help create a fore-, mid- and background to your room.

▶ Increase the horizontal lines of a room by painting stripes across the walls, or by fitting long shelving.

Creating a mood board

Often known as concept boards, mood boards are your first means to road-test your design concepts and allow you to put together the look of an idea without going to the huge expense of finishing a room before finding out you're not happy with it. They are also fun, inspiring and get you looking at colour, fabrics, furniture and magazines. The mood board can be as big as you like but it's easier if you keep it to a manageable size that you can carry around.

Once you have your board – try cardboard or foam board (compressed foam between two layers of card) bought from an art shop – one of the best places to start sourcing images is catalogues and magazines on any subject, be it interiors, fashion, nature or travel. Browse through the pages and if there are any images of interest relating to your concept that catch your eye, rip them out and pile them up. This process is often about listening to those little intuitive feelings you have about images or ideas, and acting on them.

Lay the images out on a table or the floor and, as a result of your focused attention, very often you will see a common thread linking a number of them together. If you are happy that these reflect your ideas, add them to your board; if not, keep looking. You could also take a trip out and snap some photos of anywhere that inspires you, like a bar or a club, a restaurant, a museum or a stately home.

Mood board essentials

- ► An image that represents your concept – this can be as abstract as you like
- ► A plan of the area with key dimensions, furniture and layout
- ► Paint colour samples for walls, ceiling, woodwork (such as skirting boards), floor (if it is to be painted) and additional elements such as painted furniture
- ► Fabric samples for upholstery, cushions, throws, curtains or window coverings and any other soft furnishings
- ► Lighting ideas, moods and atmospheres
- ► Floor finishes
- ► Images of key bits of furniture
- ► Any decorative details, such as stencils, or textural items
- ► Any essential styling items to complete or add to the look

The images you collate will start to tell you the sorts of colours that you should be looking for. At this stage, the best thing is to take your board to a paint shop and pick up some colour swatches to add to your board. Without your mood board to point you in the right direction this can be a daunting task. Do the same with fabrics, collecting small samples from fabric shops. You will slowly build up an idea of the complete look of the area with all aspects of the interior covered.

When you have completed your mood board, you should know where you're going. If you don't, go back to the section on concepts and ideas (pages 18–19), and check whether you've been honest with your answers!

Implementing your design

Once the creative side is nailed down, the next step is to implement your design ideas – taking them from the two dimensions of your plans and mood board to the three dimensions of your room. For this you will have to be very pragmatic, planning and costing out all the elements so that your proposed scheme can be brought within budget. You may even have to go back and choose cheaper materials, shop around a little more or be more inventive with your design until you meet that budget. This can be a difficult process, so try to decide where your priorities lie.

The best way to do this is to draw up what designers call a specification. This is basically a list of all the items required for your room – a description of what you want, the colour, size or quantity, cost (per item or per metre/yard) and where you can get it (the supplier). It is also a good idea to have an additional column for extra notes such as alternatives or lead-in times – the amount of time taken between ordering your item and its delivery. The neatest way to write your specification is to type it up as a spreadsheet on the computer. Or, if you haven't got access to a computer, draw it up as a table using squared paper.

Use your specification to be clear about your items, costs and schedule for the project. In addition, if you are undertaking a larger project, such as the design of a kitchen or bathroom you can give this specification sheet to your builder so they can get a clear idea of exactly what you want and do more concise and accurate costings for you.

Now you've got your plans, mood board and specification you will be in a much better position to go and get the items you need for your room, making your shopping trips more efficient, and not so unexpectedly expensive. Having all the necessary products and tools for your room to hand will make its creation a much faster, more enjoyable process.

Create a spreadsheet to keep all the elements needed in your room as clear and legible as possible. Create this for each space you intend to work on.

Lounge Item	Description of items included in the contract	Company	Supplier/Contact	Product specification - code, colour, spec	Quantity	Work/Lead in time	General description	Cost per item	Total Cost
Floor	Strip floor	All Floors Ltd	Brilliant floor finishes	Branston's matt varnish		3 days	Floor boards to be stripped down, stained and given 3 coats of matt varnish	250	250
Skirting boards	Paint skirting boards	D and D Decorating	M and S paint supplies	Painted white, in eggshell finish		1 day	Sand down and prepare boards and paint with two coats	100	100
Walls	Paint walls	D and D Decorating	M and S paint supplies	Vinyl matt emulsion - evening lilac		2 days	Undercoat and two top coats	450	450
Ceiling	Paint ceiling	D and D Decorating	M and S paint supplies	Vinyl matt emulsion - brilliant white		0.5 days	Two coats	70	70
Doors	Paint door	D and D Decorating	M and S paint supplies	Painted white, in eggshell finish		0.5 days	Sand down and prepare door and paint with two coats	40	40
Window frames	Paint window frames	D and D Decorating	M and S paint supplies	Painted white, in silk finish		1.5 days	Sand down and prepare frames and paint with two coats	80	80
Radiator		City Plumbing		Use existing radiator		1.5 days	Move radiator to beneath window, 850mm from hearth place wall	225	225
Electrical outlets	New electrical socket	Sparks electricians		Double socket		1 day	New double socket in hearth place wall to supply TV and video	125	125
	Fit double dimmer switch	Sparks electricians		Chrome plated		0.5 days	Replace on/off switch for chrome plated dimmer switch on wall next to door	25	25
Window dressings	Fit curtains on sliding track	MJs interiors	MJs interiors	Plastic bendable track system. Curtains Brown shot silk style 35479B		0.5 days	Buy curtains from JP's home supply shop, with sliding curtain track and fit round top of window	154	154
	Fit voile curtains	Pleats dressings	Pleats dressings	Voile drapes		0.5 days	Buy voile drapes from JP's home supply shop, fit to bottom half of window with café wire	27	27
Furniture	Sofa		MJs interiors	Alcatran 3 seater No. 325775J	1	10 weeks	Brown leather 3 seater	899	899
	Armchair		MJs interiors	Barcelona armchair No. 958679Q	1	10 weeks	Burgundy cordrouy armchair	450	450
	Floor cushions		Interior style	Large floor cushion 750mm x 750mm	2	In stock	Floor cushion in beige drill fabric	35	70
	Cushions		MJs interiors	30 x 30 cushions with covers No. 25364C	6	In stock	Cushions with covers	10	60
	Rug		MJs interiors	Strip Rug 1800mm x 1200mm	1	2 weeks	Floor rug and underlay matt 1800mm x 1200mm	250	250
	Coffee table		Antique from market	1000mm long x 400mm wide	1	To find	Dark wood retro 60s style	45	45
	Side tables		Antique from market	400mm wide x 400mm long x 450mm high	2	To find	Glass top with metal leg retro style side tables	35	70
	Shelving		Interior style	Braque - Floating style shelves	5	In stock	1500mm x 300mm wide finished in walnut veneer	25	125
	Side lights		Lovely lighting ltd	Flow light	2	In stock	Side light with plain shade and leather wrapped base	40	80
	Lamp shade		Lovely lighting ltd	Blue shade	1	In stock	Plain cylindrical shade	25	25
	Decorative lighting		Lovely lighting ltd	Fairy light	2	In stock	Fairy light in a glass vase	15	30
	Picture frames		MJs interiors	Deco frames 400mm wide x 600mm high	4	In stock	Walnut picture frames for prints	12	48
	Throw		MJs interiors	Curl wood throw	1	In stock	Throw for arm chair	35	35
	Vases		Interior style	Tricolour glass vases	3	In stock	Vases in red orange and yellow	9	27
							TOTAL COST		3760

For many people, the idea of choosing a colour scheme for a room can be quite daunting. Pure white walls are often the easiest option but to my mind, your home can be so much richer through the addition of colour.

The way in which you colour your walls will be one of the most dramatic changes to the way your room looks, so money spent on paint and wallcoverings is always money well spent for the impact it has on your space. Choosing colours can be an exciting and rewarding experience... and hey, if you don't like them, you can just change them – it's a lot easier and cheaper than buying a new sofa!

Colour can do a number of different things to your home, from creating moods and atmospheres to reflecting light and zoning spaces. It can be a lot more than just about the way the room looks. Going to your local paint shop and looking for colours can be overwhelming so it really helps to have an idea as to which direction to go in before you start looking. So where do you start?

Colour

Colour as a layer

As well as looking for inspiration for your colour scheme, there are a number of different aspects to consider besides the room concept when choosing colours. Colour is, after all, only one of several layers, together with lighting, fabrics, furniture and flooring, which affect the way your room looks. So try to consider each of these different aspects in conjunction with your room colour to get a greater sense of your overall scheme. Always start from the concept of how you want your space to be and work this idea into all aspects and decisions made in your room.

Colour and light All colours are influenced by light – the way it falls onto them and the way it reflects off them, so the orientation of your room (whether it faces, north, south, east or west) will affect your choice of colours. North-facing rooms receive no direct sunlight so the colour of the light tends to be cooler and bluer, making the room feel cold. You may want to use warmer, richer colours in these rooms to counteract this effect. Equally, south-facing rooms receive a high degree of direct sunlight, so the light is warmer and richer in tone, and to counteract this, they can be painted in cooler, lighter colours. Bear in mind that some rooms are used more by day and others more by night. If the latter is the case, remember that you may want calmer, more relaxing shades to help relieve stress at the end of a hard day.

Colour schemes The function of the room clearly affects the type of colour scheme you choose. You may wish to use calming tonal ranges of colour, more energetic complementary schemes or even to zone your space – defining different areas of a room that will contain varying functions using different areas of colour.

Tonal ranges are where you pick one colour and then go for several other colours in either a lighter or darker tone to match. The other tones can be used on the furniture, skirting boards, flooring, ceiling or window details. The overall effect is very calming as the eye enjoys the visual connection of the subtle changes of colour. This scheme can work in almost any colour but particularly in softer, relaxing tones such as browns and creams.

This page: This north-facing room receives bluer, cooler light and would benefit from warmer shades of colour. Right: This room receives warmer coloured direct sunlight so uses cooler shades of colour to keep it feeling spacious.

Above right: Tonal ranges in browns and creams create a sense of relaxing calm in this bedroom.

Complementary colour schemes are those that are created using contrasting colours that sit opposite to each other on the colour wheel (see page 30), such as blue and orange, or yellow and violet. They tend to have an energetic feel to them and produce an effect that is lively and a little more visually challenging. If you are careful when choosing the colours, complementary colour schemes can work exceptionally well.

Zoning is when the rules of complementary colour schemes are used to create areas of different activities within a space, particularly in open-plan spaces or dual-function rooms such as spare bedrooms and studies. You may want the overall colour scheme to be calm and neutral but choose a more lively colour in an area where an activity, such as working or reading, occurs, or to highlight a feature of the room, by creating a visual burst of energy.

Accent colour schemes involve using tonal ranges of basic pared-down or neutral colours then adding a few small bursts of a complementary accent colour in the form of curtains, rugs, cushions and artwork, for example. This helps you to create focus within certain rooms and may be a useful tool for rooms such as dining rooms and lounges.

Below: A complimentary scheme adds a sense of vibrancy and energy to this home office.

When you think you have made a decision about your colour scheme, but are still anxious about taking the plunge and decorating your whole room, it may be worthwhile buying matchpots of colour or the smallest amount available first and testing out the paints in your room. Remember that because of the way light falls, the same colour can look dramatically different on a wall next to the window compared with a wall opposite, so make sure you try the same colour in different areas to get a true feel of the overall effect that you will achieve. In order to do this, but avoid buying large amounts of test paints and papers, you can move the colours around by painting large pieces of paper with the colour or temporarily sticking on the types of wallpaper you wish to use. This will allow you to try out the colour scheme on different walls of your room.

Some colour terms you should know and can use to impress your friends

COMPLEMENTARY schemes use a predominance of one colour with a smaller amount of another colour that lies opposite to it on the colour wheel.

TONAL schemes use a range of the same, often neutral, colour to create a sense of calm.

ACCENT schemes use a predominance of a tonal range of colours together with small amounts of accent colours that are often bright and energetic and will add a touch of vibrancy to a space.

A HUE is another name for colour.

A TINT is your chosen colour plus some white.

A TONE is your chosen colour plus some grey.

A SHADE is your chosen colour plus some black.

Above: A block of colour has "zoned" this lounge area as a space of its own within this open plan apartment.
Right: A vibrant accent colour has created a strong visual look for this bedroom.

Choosing your colours Every day, we make dozens of basic decisions about the colour choices in our lives – from the clothes we wear to the pens we choose to write with. They are all conscious decisions that say something about us so, theoretically, choosing colour for a room should be no more difficult. The best place to start is to think about the concept of the room you are going to decorate. Do you want it to be bright and light, subdued, have a natural feel, be exciting and dynamic, or soothing? The atmosphere you wish to create will be dramatically affected by the choice of colour.

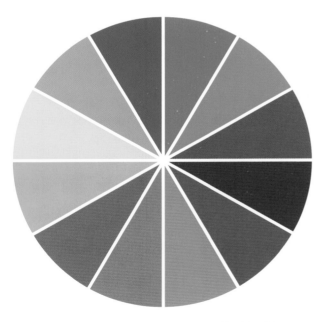

The colour wheel explains the relationship that exists between different colours and can help you to make essential colour decisions.

The colour wheel It is often suggested that the first place to start considering your colour scheme is with one of the oldest of the designer's tools – the colour wheel. This can help you pick out colours to create tonal or complementary schemes, and find accent colours that will work with your base colour. However, often so many tones and shades of colour are represented on the wheel that it becomes very difficult to pin down what is right for you. So, if you have tried the colour wheel method and it hasn't worked for you, don't worry because there are plenty of other ways to decide on the colour scheme that is right for you. It really is worth taking your time over choosing your colours as the more you start to look around you, the more you'll realize what you do and don't like.

Magazines A great place to start is magazines. Look in fashion or interiors magazines – anything with lots of photos. Glance through them and see what catches your eye; trust your intuition and your instincts and rip out images of anything you think you like, or that makes you look twice. When you've got 20 or so images, you may start to recognise they have something in common. This may be an important indicator as to the direction you are thinking of taking the colour scheme for the room. The great thing about gathering these images is that they may also indicate to you colours of other elements that you may want to add to the room, such as furniture, curtains, tables and other items like vases.

Your dress sense Getting dressed every day and the thought process that goes into it also constitutes a colour decision-making process. Think about the colour schemes of your room in a similar way and consider what sort of colours and tones you are most comfortable with. Are they bright and vibrant, or pale and muted? How do you accessorize your clothing with the likes of jewellery, cufflinks, sunglasses, watches, bags and cosmetics? In the same way, think about accessorizing your room with items such as cushions, curtains and floorcoverings that can alter the look and mood of your space from season to season, or as the mood takes you.

Familiar places In a similar light, you may want to look through holiday photos to see whether you can draw inspiration from any past experiences. Although this can give a personal look and feel to your house, be careful that you are not drawn into creating cultural pastiche – a cheap copy of a great experience. You may wish to abstract the experience you had – for example by using bold stripes of colour influenced by your holiday on a lighter base.

You may also wish to take influence from your surrounding environment. When you are out shopping or visiting a bar, café or museum, take a good look at the colours around you. Note where the colours are coming from – for example, the walls, furniture or soft furnishings – and make a mental note of how you may recreate that look at home. You can also use technology in your search for the perfect colour scheme for your room. Keep a digital camera with you at all times, then if you see a colour scheme that catches your eye, take a picture of it and take it home for consideration. This is a cheap, quick and convenient way of storing colour schemes.

Professional input Another great way of choosing colours for your room is to browse internet websites or look at brochures from paint and wallcovering companies as it is their job to sell you paint and colours. They invest a

A visual association has been made between the hearth place wall of this room, the curtains and the sofa, giving it a sense of coordination and completeness.

lot of time and energy in creating colour schemes to inspire you, as well as keeping up with the latest trends and ideas on the interiors scene.

It may also help to consider colour schemes as falling into one of the four basic categories that are used by paint companies:

▶ Calm and neutral – generally represented by tonal shades of colour or softer shades of blues, browns, beiges and whites.

▶ Warm – an easy to live with palette consisting of natural colours like reds, browns, oranges, beiges and yellows.

▶ Fresh – reflective whites used alongside with more lively, conrasting hues of colour that are often used in smaller amounts that won't dominate the main colour.

▶ Vibrant – deep, rich and bold colours, often of a more primary nature, that can be overpowering if not used carefully.

Working with existing pieces You may have already identified a colour you want to work with – perhaps because you have chosen some wallpaper that you like or have an existing piece of furniture that cannot be re-covered and needs to be incorporated into your room. If this is the case, then you should go for a base colour that is used within a surface pattern and find other colours that match in tone or shade. This will help you create a balanced and coordinated look between your walls and your furniture.

Using nature Lastly, a surefire way of finding colour schemes that work together is to look at nature for inspiration. Simply by going for a walk in the countryside or a park, you will be exposed to the colour schemes of hundreds of plants and flowers. Consider the balance of colour evident in nature. A tree, for example, may appear to be 30 per cent brown trunk, 60 per cent green leaves and 10 per cent flowering blossoms. It's this balance of base colours and accents that may be appropriate for you. Remember to look at nature's different scales too, from macro to micro, from rolling green hills to the moss on the side of a stone. There is little more powerful than nature to inspire your colour schemes, providing that you know where to look.

Using nature to inspire your scheme will inevitably create colour schemes that are successful.

Light and colour

Colour is all about light reflection. Without light, there is no colour so how you treat the lighting in your room will obviously have a dramatic effect on the colours. As I've already mentioned, the orientation of your room will affect the way that you see colours. Similarly, the way you light your room affects the colours. Bear in mind that different types of lighting provide different colours (see 'Lightbulbs', pages 52–5). For example, standard tungsten bulbs have a warm, yellow colour rendering, whereas fluorescent lighting has a cold, green quality. So, if you cannot alter the artificial lighting in your room, bear in mind that you may wish to adjust your colour scheme accordingly to accommodate the light.

When considering the atmosphere you want in your room, remember that some colours are much more reflective than others. White obviously reflects the most light so painting a room completely white allows you to bounce the maximum amount of available light around the room. Although this may seem like an advantageous situation, this amount of light can be an absolute mood-killer, so consider using white in specific areas only, like window mullions (the vertical struts dividing panes of glass from one another) and sills. With these

areas painted white, light will travel through the window and bounce off their reflective surfaces and into the room. The same light can then be bounced in further again if the ceiling is also painted white.

The control of light plays an important role in creating a romantic atmosphere – think of the warm flickering light of a candle falling onto someone's face. In this scenario, light travels from a single source point onto the face. In contrast, in a bright, white room, light is bounced off a variety of different surfaces,

giving a much more even and less romantic sense of light. So, if you are after a romantic room, you may wish to colour the walls of your space in darker shades in order to control the light coming from a single source point – be it from the window or artificial lights in the room.

Above: A variety of lights have been used to create a sense of mood, atmosphere and function in this bedroom.

TIPS:

► You may wish to accentuate the lines of your room with bands of colour. Horizontal lines increase the sense of length of an area, converging lines increase perspective, while vertical lines increase light and space and draw your eye up to the ceiling.

► There is currently a resurgence in the popularity of wallpaper as a decorative feature in people's homes. You can create a sophisticated and intelligent look by using wallpaper on a single focus wall and picking out a colour from it and then using a tonal range of that colour across the rest of the room.

► To create tonal ranges of paint, simply buy your chosen colour and add quantities of either white or black to it to change its tone. Small quantities of black will change the tone more obviously than large quantities of white, which will in effect pale the colour out.

► When decorating your room, it makes sense to start with the ceiling and work your way down the walls to the floor. However, you may wish to complete the flooring first, especially if you are sanding it, and then cover it up to protect it from paint.

► If you are using stronger colours in a room, a good way to keep the space feeling fresh and light is to paint the skirting board and window mullions in white. Often, this band of white will allow you to separate colours and use contrasting ones next to each other.

► For a more intense coordinated feel, paint details such as the window mullions and skirting board in the same colours or darker or lighter tonal shades of the wall colour. This will create a more intense feel, which can be perfect for areas such as romantic bedrooms.

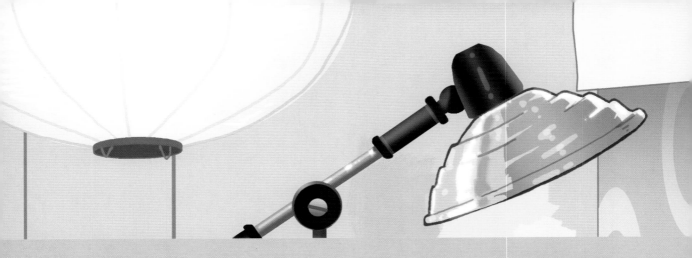

After colour, the single most important decorative feature in your home is lighting. It is an incredibly versatile medium that carries out a variety of different functions in your home. Its high degree of flexibility allows you to transform spaces at the flick of a switch and it can provide you with more options in your home than any other element. Stop for a moment and consider what light can do for us... It allows us to see colour and shade, and can help create mood and atmosphere. Artificial lighting allows us to carry out tasks such as preparing food and reading; lighting in the office can make you feel wide awake or drowsy, while a pool of light can draw you to an object or area. The flickering light of a fire will fascinate your attention in a primeval way, while sunlight determines our daily routines – we sleep when it's dark and are awake during the day.

Lighting

Working with light Light is a powerful medium and can be used in a variety of ways around the home. Good lighting creates focus, makes the home safer, allows you to zone areas, creates atmosphere and even helps prevent eye strain. It's good fun to experiment with different effects and types of lighting to see what suits your needs.

Lighting is one of the easiest and cheapest elements to adapt and change in your home – it's a great solution for instant change on a budget – and it has the greatest impact on the look and practicality of your rooms. However, it helps to follow the rules and consider all the different types of lighting for every area in your home. There are five basic types to be aware of: natural light, general lighting, task lighting, accent lighting and decorative lighting.

Five basic types of lighting

▶ **Natural light** The most abundant form of lighting in any home is natural daylight. It's a dynamic form of light that changes position and even colour throughout the day, having a dramatic effect on our sense of wellbeing and routine. It's a good idea to maximize the potential daylight opportunities of each room.

▶ **General lighting** Also known as ambient lighting, this provides the general level of illumination in the room. In many houses, this is provided by a central ceiling-mounted pendant but it could come from a variety of other sources.

▶ **Task lighting** This is the lighting required in order to carry out activities safely and without straining your eyes. It is frequently used in practical areas such as kitchens, bathrooms and studies. In general, it is a relatively small light cast directly onto the area where you may be cooking, shaving, working, reading or writing.

▶ **Accent lighting** This lighting is used to highlight specific features of your home. It is generally a spotlight shone directly onto an object like a painting, a bookshelf or even an architectural feature within your home, such as a niche or decorative moulding.

▶ **Decorative lighting** This is the lighting used to create mood and atmosphere. Generally, these are lights that throw out very little illumination and are purely decorative, for example fairy lights or candles.

Natural light Throughout the day, your home – assuming it has windows like most houses – is subject to the effects of the earth rotating around the sun. This creates an ever-changing natural light that dramatically affects the atmosphere in a room – this natural light brings your room to life.

Look at the orientation of your house and the rooms within it and consider how natural daylight affects these spaces. The sun rises in the east, bringing with it the early morning light, which has a warm, orangey feel that is naturally invigorating. As the sun rises higher into the sky, we get daylight with a cooler, bluer quality. The sun sets in the west and the light reverts to warmer, orange hues again.

These colour differences have a dramatic effect on the atmosphere of the rooms of your home and can be further manipulated by the use of different colours within these rooms. In rooms that receive direct sunlight, you may want to counteract the warm light by using cooler colours, whereas in rooms that receive no direct sunlight, you may want to use warmer colours such as reds, yellows and oranges in the fabrics and paints in order to give the room a more inviting feel.

Maximizing the available light Whatever the orientation of your room, it is a good idea to make the best use of the available light that you have. This will give your room a greater sense of energy during the day, and will also reduce your electricity bill by cutting down on the amount of artificial light required.

There are a number of ways in which you can maximize the amount of natural light in a room. Firstly, consider the windows or openings that allow the natural light in. Make sure these are clean – it is surprising how much dirty windows can affect the amount of natural light entering a room. Try to ensure that you don't block the window in an unnecessary way with window coverings such as large draped curtains, which can reduce the window surface area by up to one-third. In addition, cut back as much as possible any natural obstructions outside, such as bushes or hedges that restrict the light entering the room.

Natural light is allowed to flood into this dining area but can be carefully controlled through the use of adjustable Venetian blinds.

Secondly, remember that light bounces and can be reflected into a room from a variety of surfaces. By painting your window frames, sills and surrounds in brilliant white, you can provide surfaces for light to bounce off and into the room. This idea will extend to floors, walls and ceilings – lighter, shiny glossy surfaces will reflect a greater amount of light into the space.

Lastly, you can use features such as mirrors and polished tables as surfaces that will bounce light into a room or reflect what light is already there. This may mean positioning a table or a mirror near a window and allowing its shiny surface to act as a reflector. When positioned at the darkest end of a room, mirrors can also reflect and double the amount of light that is available.

Retaining privacy If privacy is an issue in your room, try to find ways to obscure vision without blocking out all the natural light. You could fit opaque or textured glass, use lightweight sheer fabrics as curtains or even spray glass etch (a glass frosting spray paint available from good do-it-yourself and craft

Left: Light has been bounced around
this bathroom by the white walls,
reflective surfaces and mirrors.
Above and right: Blinds that pull up
vertically using a simple pulley system
retain privacy but will still allow
views up to the sky.

stores) over the window glass, although you should be aware that this can produce a patchy effect unless you apply several layers. A better option is to use a self-adhesive plastic film that gives a frosted-glass effect. This is available from most glaziers or do-it-yourself stores. If it is not necessary to block off the whole window to create privacy, try obscuring just the bottom half. This will allow more light to enter the room through the clear glass at the top of the window. A more permanent way of creating the same effect is by using a roller blind mounted on the windowsill; with a simple

system of pulleys, you can raise the blind to the desired height and tie it off using hooks as and when required.

To make more of any available light that comes from a window in a neighbouring area like a hallway, a good option is to replace your solid doors with glass panelled ones. This allows the light to seep from one room into another area, while retaining a sense of privacy. If you do decide to do this, make sure that you use toughened glass and check that you are not replacing a fire door with a product of a lower standard.

General lighting This is the light that illuminates the entire area of a room rather than specific parts. It is the most important light in any space and should therefore be the first that you consider. The most common, and the most inefficient, form of general lighting is the single pendant light hanging in the middle of the room. This type of light illuminates the general floor area of the space but inevitably, all the activities that you carry out in the room are around its edge and are therefore generally undertaken with a shadow falling on you. It is a much better idea to think about a series of smaller lights that will provide a far more even spread of illumination across the entire floor area. There are a variety of ways in which you can do this...

Ceiling-mounted downlighters In recent years, ceiling-mounted downlighters, such as halogens or spotlights, have become popular and efficient ways to create an even, general light across a room. Set in a basic grid system across the ceiling and operated by an ordinary or dimmer switch, they result in low levels of light being cast evenly across the room. Although this is still thought to be the best system, bear in mind that you will have more bulbs to replace more frequently and the initial installation costs are higher. This is because you will need an electrician to fit this system, who will either have to cut into the ceiling to fit the lights or, if possible, pull up the flooring from the floor above in order to do a proper job. If this is not possible, then it is worth considering one of the other forms of general lighting for your space.

Cable-mounted halogen lights Made popular in the 1990s, cable-mounted low-voltage halogen lights are still a favourite option for general lighting in a room, although some people consider them a little dated. The great thing about them is that you don't have to cut into the ceiling to install them; they are quick and easy to fit and very flexible once in use – you can move them easily to create a good, even spread of light across the whole room according to your needs or the room's layout. In addition, they come in a massive variety of designs and shapes, which can add a style statement to your room. The cost of the initial fitting is low as it can be a simple do-it-yourself project, but the expense of replacing the bulbs make this a costly option in the long run.

Ceiling-mounted pendants If you have the chance to fit ceiling-mounted pendant lights in your space, remember that positioning them centrally is the most inefficient way to provide light. It is much better to place several of them across the ceiling area so they light the area evenly. With ceiling-mounted pendant lights you can choose the lampshade of your choice, allowing the opportunity for personalization and the creation of your individual look. In addition, you can use low-energy, long-life lightbulbs, which will help reduce your electricity bill and need replacing far less often than conventional bulbs. The only downside to energy-efficient bulbs is that the light they provide can be quite a cold blue, so try to pick lampshades that will conceal the bulb and tint the light emitted by it with a slightly warmer colour.

If your only option is to use a centrally-mounted pendant light as your main general light, consider fitting it with a long cable that will allow you to hook the light up from the ceiling in different areas of the room when necessary. You could even get an electrician to fit two or three cables from the same light fitting. This will allow you to drape lights across the ceiling to hang in different corners of the room.

Uplighters Generally wall-mounted or freestanding, uplighters throw light upwards so as to bounce it off a surface such as a wall or ceiling to give a soft, even spread of light. In order to do this, the bulbs generally have to be of a high wattage as light is reduced when it bounces off a surface. Bear in mind that when you bounce light off a surface, the colour of that surface will affect the light bouncing into the room. It works well if you are bouncing light off a white ceiling, for example, but poorly from a dark-coloured wall. Uplighters often use high-wattage bulbs, such as halogen or tungsten, which create large amounts of heat and can collect dust. When the dust burns off, it may create an unpleasant aroma in the room (and you don't even want to think about the dead flies!). Unless your uplighters are on stands based on the floor, the lights will have to be wired up by an electrician, who will cut a channel in the wall to hide the cables. These channels will then need to be plastered over to conceal the cables. Uplighters are therefore an effective choice for the general lighting of a room but can be costly to install and relatively expensive to maintain. Again, fitting dimmer switches to uplighters allows you to create a softer mood within your room.

Alternatively, if you already have a ceiling mounted pendant, but want to soften the light that comes from it, you could try fitting an uplighting ceiling pendant. This will reflect light both direcly onto the ceiling and from the shade itself. Another interesting product that you can try experimenting with is the crown-silvered bulb. These tungsten lights have a mirrored base that reflects light, creating intimate pools of light and cutting glare and light spillage.

Fluorescent strip lighting Due to the cold, harsh green light produced by fluorescent tubes and the fact that you cannot dim them to soften the effect, they are not generally appropriate for the interior of the home. The only way to use fluorescent tubes effectively here is to cover them with a heatproof coloured gel or purpose-made coloured sleeve to warm up the colour of the bulb and to conceal the entire light fitting so it will not produce visual glare. The effects of this can be exciting as the glow produced from the fluorescent tube is soft and even. Positioned above cupboards in a kitchen, it can bounce light across the ceiling, or positioned under furniture like wardrobes, it can produce the effect that the piece is floating. If you live in a house where strip lights are fitted and you can't change them, you could consider using freestanding uplighters as an alternative or, if possible, creating a perforated cover to reduce the harsh effect of the light that comes off the fluorescent tube.

Wall-mounted lights In a similar way to uplighters, wall-mounted general lights need to be fitted carefully – probably by an electrician, who will need either to chase a channel in the wall to take the cables or to fit the cables within a surface-mounted conduit (a plastic or metal tube) for a more industrial look. To achieve good general lighting from wall-mounted lights, you need to position a series of lights around the room to provide an even spread of light across the whole area. Hence, the installation cost of wall-mounted general lights can be expensive, but the variety of lights on the market means it is possible to fit energy-efficient long-life lightbulbs to make the running costs economical.

Task lighting As the name suggests, task lighting illuminates areas where particular activities take place. This has different applications in different rooms of the home – for instance, in a kitchen, you need task lights above a work surface to aid in the preparation and cooking of food. In a lounge, you may require a task light to read by and in a bedroom you may need a light to help you choose the clothes you want to wear. Task lighting can make an area safe and more efficient to work in and may also help prevent eye strain, which occurs when the eye is made to operate in areas with dramatically different levels of light. For instance, if you are working by night at a computer screen and the light level around you is very low, your eyes will constantly have to adjust between the brightness of the screen and the darkness around it. Well thought-out task lights, when used in addition to general lights, can help provide a balanced, level lighting scheme for rooms where activity takes place. Luckily there is a wide choice available – for every conceivable style of room.

Fluorescent tube task lights These are generally used to cast light in bathrooms, kitchens or the interiors of cupboards. The light is diffused and comes from a wide source point (across the tube), which reduces harsh shadows, making it an efficient task light. In areas where water is involved, such as bathrooms or kitchens, make sure that your fluorescent tube light is protected in such a way that it is not possible to touch any of the electrical fittings. When buying these lights, check they are designed for the purpose you intend. The cold quality of the light provided by fluorescent tubes means they are not suitable for areas of relaxation, such as lounges or bedrooms.

Halogen lights Individually mounted halogen lights are often used as an efficient way to create task lighting in the kitchen or bathroom. Although relatively cheap to purchase, halogen lights throw light from a single source point so create harsh shadows. In addition, the bulbs do not have a long life span so are costly to maintain.

Table lamps/side lights There are a massive variety of such lights available. They generally comprise a light with a stand and shade and a switch located along the length of the cord. They are useful for creating pools of light in areas such as bedrooms and lounges and providing you get a lampshade that is wide enough, can be used to read by. In addition to providing task lighting, they also add atmosphere and character to a room and can be useful for warming up a cold, dark corner.

Desk lamps/angle-poise lamps Again, there are a massive variety on offer, but these lights generally have a solid base and a stand with the lightbulb shielded or directed by the shade. It's important to pick for your work area a light with a shade that will prevent glare from the lightbulb, which can potentially create eye strain. Try to choose a desk lamp with some level of flexibility, such as an angle-poise lamp, which allows you to manipulate it into a variety of positions to best suit the task you are carrying out – for example, to shine light on to a surface or on to a wall to balance the lighting levels.

Clip-on lights These are very simple lampshades with lightbulbs and a large oversized clip. They are quick and easy to fit and can be very inexpensive, so are very convenient. Just plug them in, clip them on to a horizontal or vertical surface and you're ready to go. Just make sure the cable doesn't get in the way of what you are doing.

Wall-mounted lights These are generally used where furniture is unlikely to move, such as behind the headboard in the bedroom. Being fixed to the wall, they look slick but can be costly to install as the cables need to be concealed behind the plasterwork.

Standard lamps These are generally tall lamps with solid bases, which plug into the nearest electrical socket. They are great for shining light over your shoulder while you sit in your favourite chair and read. There are a large number of lights in different styles and materials on offer. If chosen carefully, they will add an air of elegance and sophistication to your room.

Torches and candles OK, so they are not normally regarded as task lights but when the power fails, they will be all you have! It's a really good idea to put torches and candles in a memorable and easy-to-reach location like a bedside table or kitchen drawer. Torches are also invaluable when searching for objects in dark, unlit cupboards, such as under the stairs.

Accent lighting Accent lighting can be used to highlight points of architectural or decorative interest in your home and allows you to create a sense of character and personality through your lighting scheme. It can be used to illuminate anything from bookshelves and pieces of furniture to sculptures and paintings, or even unusual architectural features in your home.

Feature lighting can be particularly useful in hallways when there is often little extra space other than the walls to create interest. Feature lights can be ceiling-mounted spotlights, wall-mounted down- or uplighters, or even recessed lights positioned in furniture such as display cabinets. In general, they are fixed lights that require installation by an electrician, although careful use of angle-poise or clip-on lamps (using mirrored spotlight bulbs) can do the trick, provided you hide unsightly cables.

Accent lighting makes the most of this striking display in an otherwise simple entrance hallway.

Decorative lighting

For me, decorative lighting is by far and away the most enjoyable type of lighting to think about as it incorporates anything from a roaring log fire or a string of fairy lights to a series of night-light candles. It is wonderful for creating mood and atmosphere in a room. To create the right level it can be a good idea to start off in the dark (with your torch, of course) and then turn on small lights across the room until you create the perfect lighting environment. Good decorative lighting will dramatically improve your chances in romantic situations or simply aid relaxation after a stressful day at work!

Decorative lights are great fun and easy to use to create different moods. They can be the cheapest form of decorative accessory to your room and range from a simple candle to twinkling fibreoptic systems or even chandeliers fitted with a dimmer switch (see box opposite).

Fairy lights The humble string of fairy lights has a variety of uses and is sometimes best displayed with a little imagination. Fairy lights are quick and easy to use and, above all, cheap to buy. Here are a few ways of creating decorative lighting with a string of fairy lights:
► Coil up fairy lights in a glass or frosted glass vase.
► Drill a board of MDF (medium-density fibreboard) with holes in a pattern of your choice. Working from behind the board, fit each individual bulb into a separate hole, concealing the cable but creating a panel of lights to hang on your wall.
► Wrap fairy lights around features in your home, such as columns or a stair balustrade for a magical effect.
► Position fairy lights in an empty fireplace or around logs to create a summertime fireplace installation.
► Wrap a string of lights around painted twigs for a sense of wintry fairytale warmth.

Remember, fairy lights can get hot so make sure that you don't wrap them in inflammable materials like cloth and don't prevent air circulating around the bulbs, which helps them to stay cool.

Remember that fairy lights are not just for Christmas – they are fun, frivolous and look great at night.

Decorative lights to consider

- ► Candles
- ► Strings of fairy lights
- ► Net lights (a cargo net of wires with bulbs at every junction)
- ► Rope lights (plastic-covered strings of pulsating lights)
- ► Table lamps with shades
- ► Domestic fibreoptic lighting systems
- ► Lava lamps
- ► Plastic furniture-sized, polypropylene plastic lights
- ► Colour-changing LED (light-emitting diode) rechargeable lights – destined to become the lights of the future

Lightbulbs There are a variety of different types of lightbulb available, all with different functions and emitting a different colour of light. Before you go out and spend your money, it's useful to know what your options are.

Tungsten bulbs and tubes Tungsten bulbs are the conventional lightbulbs used today and have remained relatively unchanged since their invention. The colour rendering from these bulbs has a warm, yellow quality, which becomes much warmer and more orange when dimmed. Tungsten bulbs add a sense of warmth to your room but are energy and cost inefficient due to the heat that they create and their relatively short life span. Although they are cheap to buy, you will need to replace them fairly regularly. Tungsten strip lights give off a diffused light and are an alternative to the longer fluorescent tube. In addition, they can be fitted with dimmer switches so they may be used to create mood and atmosphere.

Tungsten bulbs come in a variety of sizes (standard, pygmy), shapes (standard, candle, golf ball) and fittings (screw-in or bayonet), so make sure that you buy the right type. In addition, you can get clear bulbs, which create a harsh light but beautiful shadows, pearlized bulbs for a softer, more diffused feel, or mirrored bulbs, which bounce or focus light. They also come in a variety of different colours – soft tones to warm the atmosphere of a room, or stronger colours like blues, reds and greens, which can dramatically alter the mood in your home and are great for creating atmosphere if you're having a party.

If you are doing a task that requires accurate colour rendering, you can buy 'daylight correction' bulbs, which mimic the colour of natural daylight and make colours appear truer than they would under the yellowy light of a standard tungsten bulb. These are more expensive than standard bulbs but are worth it for the accuracy of light. They can normally be bought from good art materials, craft and lighting stores.

Energy-saving bulbs The environmentally friendly option, these are likely to be the main choice of lightbulb in the future. Although more expensive to buy than conventional tungsten bulbs, energy-saving bulbs use the same fittings, consume far less electricity and will last a staggering 12 times longer. Hence they will actually pay for themselves in terms of reduced electricity bills and replacement costs in just six months.

Due to the colour rendering of energy-saving bulbs you should use warm-coloured lampshades to give their light a warmer quality.

Halogen bulbs Generally, these are small bulbs that clip simply into a fitting. They are now commonplace around the home and can be bought at all electrical or do-it-yourself shops. The light they produce has a good colour rendering, similar to daylight, and so they are useful in a variety of

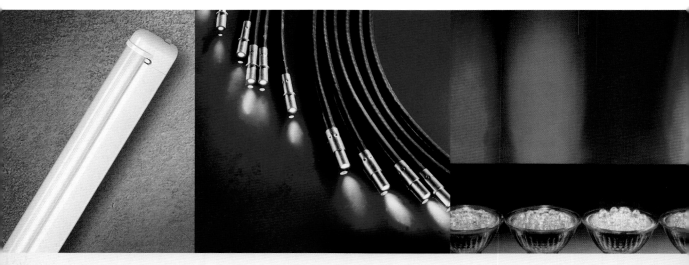

situations such as bathrooms, kitchens and general lighting. They have a relatively short life span and are more expensive to replace than conventional bulbs. The light they produce is quite sharp as it comes from a single source point and has a tendency to create harsh shadows.

Halogen bulbs come in high- and low-voltage forms. The former can be fitted with dimmer switches in a variety of situations; the low-voltage variety need to be fitted with a transformer but can be used to great decorative effect – for example, if strung on cables across the room.

Fluorescent tubes These tend to come in specific standard lengths and have bulky fittings to make them work. The light they produce tends to have a high green content, which is not flattering on the skin, so they are best used in activity areas such as garages or workrooms.

Fibreoptics At one time expensive and difficult to obtain, there are now domestic fibreoptic systems, which are very cheap and easy to use in a variety of situations where small pinpoints of pulsating or static light are required. The system consists of a small light box about the size of a shoebox with a number of black fibreoptic cables coming out of it. Each cable transmits light from the box to its end and can be fitted through surfaces such as ceilings or panels.

Fibreoptics are a great option for decorative lighting in bathrooms, bedrooms and lounges. The best way to source them is to ask in a lighting shop or to carry out an internet search.

LED lighting Light-emitting diodes (LED) are likely to become the lighting of the future. The bulbs, which are the same as those used in the new generation of bicycle lights, are small, cheap, very efficient and have an extremely long life span. In addition, they come in a variety of colours and will eventually take over from other sorts of lighting within the home.

TIPS:

If you must have a pendant light in the centre of the room, replace the on/off switch with a dimmer. This will allow you to balance the lighting levels in the room with other lights such as task and feature lights to create more energetic or more relaxing atmospheres.

When choosing lights for areas that contain water such as bathrooms and kitchens, make sure they have the correct safety rating so that it is not possible for water or steam to touch any electrical element. Your salesman should be able to advise you as to which lights are appropriate for your needs.

Always be careful with lights and electricity as it is very easy to electrocute yourself. If you are installing or fixing any electrical appliance, always turn off the power at the fuse box first. Better still, call a qualified electrician.

Use a variety of lights to give your room flexibility and character – natural light for vibrancy, general light for practicality, task lighting for functional use and decorative lighting for mood.

How you deal with your walls and ceilings will have a large impact on the overall style of a room, affecting the atmosphere, light and even the sense of space within it. Walls and ceilings are one of the fundamental building blocks of your style – they offer an opportunity to turn a bland featureless space into one with character and focus. Think of them not just as flat planes but consider the sense of composition and layering that they demonstrate – consider colour, detail (such as stencilling), shelving, other elements hung on the wall, light washing across from the window and furniture positioned in front of them.

Wall finishes

Thinking it through Your choice of how to treat your walls will force you to consider the relationship you want between the surfaces and the overall space in general. Although this may seem like an odd idea it is worth considering a few possibilities.

- ► Do you want plain blocks of colour or to break up stronger lines?
- ► Do you want to use the walls to bounce light into the room?
- ► Are there any features that you wish to emphasize or to hide?
- ► Will the room need a textural input like wallpaper or stencilling? If so, where will it best create a focus?
- ► Do you want to display items like pictures or objects on the wall, and how will your décor frame these objects?
- ► Do you have any other functional requirements for the wall, such as pin boards or mirrors?
- ► Do you want to change the sense of proportion of the wall using a dado rail or stripes of colour?

You get a real sense of the character of this home's occupants through the ways they have used their walls.

It can be a good idea when you first move in to paint all the walls white so that you get an understanding of the potential light and to freshen up the place. However, it is often a missed opportunity to leave them this way and not explore the possibilities offered by treating your walls with a variety of other decorative finishes or colours.

Preparing your walls Although it may seem like a slow and tedious job, the quality of finish of your walls and ceilings will depend very much on the level of preparation that you put into it. A poorly prepared wall may not accept the wall finish – paper or paint will just peel away – and rough plaster or unsanded filler simply looks shabby and unloved. So, if you want to show that you love your home, you need to put in the groundwork.

Start by stripping back all the existing paper on the walls or, if they are painted, any loose paint. You can strip off old wallpaper using just hot water and a scraper, but it is really much more advisable to hire or buy a steam wallpaper stripper. The paper will just fall away, allowing you to complete the task in a quarter of the time. Next, give the walls a light wash with hot water and sugar soap to remove any leftover particles and grease that will have an effect on the final finish.

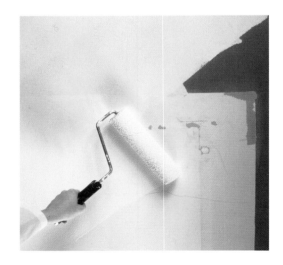

If wood surfaces such as windowsills and skirting boards have several layers of old paint it can be a good idea to strip these back. Although this is a real labour of love, just think how much you will appreciate the crisp quality finish. Again, if you can find ways to make this easier – just do them! Try hiring or buying a heat gun to scorch off the paint or use a chemical paint stripper to peel away the layers. You can use a drill with a wire brush stripper although this may damage the wood beneath. Generally, any surface that is to receive an eggshell or gloss paint needs to be primed with the appropriate undercoat. Surfaces that may be taking emulsion (water-based paint) are less likely to need an undercoat, although undercoats can be used to fill in hairline cracks and cover old colours.

Next, check over the entire surface of the walls and ceiling looking for cracks, dents and holes that need filling using a paste filler and a scraper. If the holes are very big, fill them in a series of layers or fill the bulk of the cavity with rolled-up newspaper before using paste filler. If a section of plaster comes away from the wall it may be necessary to get in a plasterer to reskim the exposed surface with a fresh layer of plaster – this is one of those jobs that really is harder than it looks to do well.

Once the filler is thoroughly dry, sand the patch flat so that it is flush with the surrounding wall. If larger cracks, which have already been filled, reappear, get a structural engineer to undertake a survey (see 'Calling in professionals', page 231) as this may indicate a structural problem, which could lead to more drastic measures being required.

Providing you have no structural cracks in your wall, your room will now be ready for decorating.

How to deal with a textured ceiling

A frequent question is how to remove the textured plaster ceilings that were once a common decorative feature, and are now largely seen as a style mistake. The surfaces are tough and sharp and almost impossible to do anything with other than paint, which is also a nightmare as you cannot use a roller and brushwork is slow and laborious. The ceiling can also sometimes contain dangerous fibres that should not be disturbed, so by no means should you try to sand the texture away.

Although they are a time-consuming, labour-intensive task to deal with, there are several solutions to the problem. Most are very hard work but almost certainly worth it!

▶ Soften the surface with a steam stripper before using a wide-bladed scraper on it. Once stripped, lightly wash down the area. Repeat this process until the ceiling is clear of textured plaster.

▶ Apply a specialized textured paint remover liquid, which will release the texture surface to be removed by the scraper. Be sure to wear adequate protective clothing – eye goggles, dust mask and long gloves – to prevent the stripper from getting onto your skin.

▶ There are lots of products available in the form of thick plaster-style paints, requiring no plastering skills, that can be applied if the texture is not too pronounced. Ask at your local do-it-yourself or hardware store for information.

▶ The last, most costly method is to get a plasterer to skim a layer of fresh, smooth finishing plaster over the ceiling, particularly if the texture is quite pronounced. The only problem with this method is that the additional weight of plaster could potentially overload the strength of the ceiling. If you have any doubts, consult a structural engineer, builder or plasterer.

Paint One of the most obvious solutions to wall decoration, paint offers a massive range of colours and there is a surprising variety to choose from. In addition, the skills needed for painting can be easily mastered. Even relatively complex decorative techniques may be learnt easily and experimented with until perfected. The materials and tools needed are widely available and, once completed, the effects can be dramatic and satisfying. Paints are either water-based, such as emulsion, or oil-based, like eggshell or gloss.

Water-based paints Emulsion is suitable for covering areas like walls and ceilings, but is not very hardwearing so cannot be wiped down without harming the surface. You usually need at least two coats to give the wall a flat ,even surface colour. Emulsion is generally a relatively low-odour paint and is suitable for painting bedrooms but look at the labelling to check the VOC (volatile organic compound) level. VOCs are gases emitted by some paints, which can be toxic if ingested, hence they are not suitable for rooms such as bedrooms and kitchens or anywhere with poor ventilation.

The quality and coverage of the paint will be affected by the quality of the ingredients. It is sometimes a false economy to buy cheaper emulsions, which require more time and paint to achieve the same level of coverage as more expensive paints.

Above: For a smooth, flat finish use emulsion (water based paint) on your walls where they won't get too much wear.
Above right: Use gloss or eggshell paint in areas of high wear – it is tough enough to take knocks and can be washed down.

Oil-based paints Oil-based paints are available in different types of finish like matt, eggshell or gloss, and often come in colours to match those of your emulsion paints if so desired. Oil-based paints are tougher and therefore suitable for harder-wearing areas like windowsills and skirting boards, allowing you to wipe these surfaces down without deteriorating the surface.

Oil-based paints need a higher degree of preparation to get a decent result. You will need a priming coat on a bare wood or metal surface, or you will need to 'key' a previously painted surface by sanding it with fine sandpaper or electric sander. Gloss paints tend to highlight any dents in the surface, and also attract dust, so are much harder to finish well. Matt or eggshell paints, however, hide surface blemishes to give a more professional final finish while being just as durable.

Gloss and oil-based paints tend to have higher VOC levels so should be minimized in areas like bedrooms, which have long periods of occupancy. A good option may be to investigate one of the many new organic paints on the market – carry out an internet search to find your nearest supplier, or try contacting Friends of the Earth. Made from natural materials, the paint comes in a softer, more natural palette of colours and has a much less noticeable smell, resulting in no headaches and a good night's sleep.

Above: There are a variety of paint effects that will give
your walls texture, just don't go over board with them!
Right: A wide and exciting range of stencils are available
to add a unique decorative touch to your space, so don't
be limited.

Paint effects Besides painting your walls in plain blocks of colour there are a vast number of techniques for paint effects. These can add visual interest and texture to your walls but tend to go in and out of fashion – ragging and sponging saw their heyday in the 1980s, for example – so be careful how often you use them in your home. Practise the technique first on a board or a length of lining paper before starting on your walls so that your learning process isn't played out on your final wall decoration. Techniques like marbling and graining in particular take some time to master. This will also allow you to check that you like the colour combination. Paint effects generally work best when there are only subtle differences in the choices of colour – for example rag a base coat with a colour that is only two shades lighter. Also consider the proportions of the area to paint as it may be a good idea to cover only certain areas of a wall.

Stencilling Many people have a fixed idea that stencilling can look a little twee and too delicate for their tastes. However, I urge you to think again and to look a little further into this method as there are amazing possibilities other than decorative fleurs-de-lis.

Creating a stencil is all about learning what to cut out and what to leave in place. You can easily make your own stencil by putting a photo or image on a photocopier and altering the darkness/lightness button. This will bleed the light and make your editing decisions for you. You can then trace these lines onto some thick stencilling card in order to cut out and make your own stencil. You can create stencils of city skylines, flowers, shells, faces, planes or even little animals. It is an opportunity to have fun with repeated decorative elements and to make a space personal to you. Alternatively, you can hire or buy ready-made stencils. They come in a massive variety of styles so you will certainly find something exciting to use.

As an alternative to stencilling, or if you want to create something on a bigger scale, get hold of an overhead or slide projector and project your chosen image onto a wall. Draw around the image on the wall and then decide how to paint it. You could make the image abstract by painting it in three shades of your existing wall colour or even try a contrasting one. This is a great way to make a large graphic statement without being a highly trained artist.

Wallpaper

Wallpaper As a wall finish, wallpaper has dropped in popularity in recent years, partly as a reaction to the overdecorated styles of the 1970s, partly due to the parental view of it as being the only material with which to cover your walls, and partly because of the time and effort required to hang it.

However, wallpaper is now making a comeback. There are contemporary styles on the market and it is used in a more sparing, intelligent way. Many high-street stores are also relaunching traditional styles and some are reinventing old ones, encouraging us to reintroduce texture and pattern back into our lives. Wallpaper, it must be said, should be used thoughtfully – not only for cost purposes, but also to optimize its dramatic effect. A little patterned paper can add texture, colour and life to a room, but could be overpowering if used to cover the entire space. So instead, think about using pattern to create focus, drawing the eye to a particular part of the room, or away from an unsightly feature. In a lounge the feature wall may surround the fireplace; in a bedroom it may be the wall behind the bed. You can combine this texture with painted walls, picking out the paint colour from the tones in the wallpaper.

There are a wide variety of different styles of wallpaper available and choosing one can be difficult, particularly if you are inexperienced at choosing pattern. So take your time and, if possible, narrow down your selection by taking sample pieces back home, pinning them to your wall and matching them with an additional paint colour.

Printed papers These are the most common types of wallpaper and are machine printed. They come in a wide range of colours and styles, are relatively strong and easy to use. Printed papers are available from most do-it-yourself stores, but do shop around for the more beautiful ones. Hand block-printed papers are very expensive due to the labour involved and are weaker when wet, so should be handled carefully. The inks have a tendency to run when glue touches them and the patterns can be tricky to line up, so these papers should really be hung by professionals.

Embossed papers These are thick, heavy papers with patterns stamped, or embossed, into the surface. They can be very hardwearing so are useful in hallways, but are also great for adding subtle texture to a room. Generally white, they are painted once hung on the wall. In areas of high wear it can be a good idea to use a paint that will be tough enough to wipe away marks and scuffs. Using a gloss or silk finish paint will allow light to reflect off the paper, and highlight the embossed surface pattern.

Washable and vinyl papers Most suitable for kitchens and bathrooms, these are printed papers with a thin waterproof layer of PVA or vinyl, which allows you to wipe the surface down. They are very hardwearing but cannot be painted over. Whilst these sound like a great idea on the whole they have not manage to move with the times, and their range of styles and designs can be limited, so you will need to search hard for one that you like.

Natural fibre papers These papers comprise a variety of natural fibres, such as hessian, dried grasses and cork, which are woven into a mesh and glued to a paper backing. Although providing a soft but striking natural feel, they are delicate, expensive and difficult to wipe down, so best used in areas where they are unlikely to get damaged.

Flock wallpapers Flock wallpapers have a main pattern picked out in a short-pile velvet on a background comprising the surface of the paper. This is a traditional-style paper, a fact often reflected by intricate Victorian-style patterns. Although flock wallpapers can seem overpowering, they may work very well in small amounts in older-style properties – for example, to create a focus.

Wall tiles As with floor tiles there are a massive variety of wall tiles to choose from. They are hardwearing, water- and heatproof, easy to wipe down and can be cut into smaller pieces to fit into awkward spaces. Tiling is a slightly challenging but very satisfying do-it-yourself project to undertake. The final result lasts a long time and makes the effort put into the job worthwhile. Tiles basically fall into four types: ceramic (glazed and unglazed), mosaic and quarry tiles.

Ceramic tiles Glazed ceramic tiles have a tough impermeable layer that repels dirt and water. They can be either hand or machine made, a factor that affects both the price and the regularity of size. Ceramic tiles are generally square in shape, although rectangular tiles are available and may add interest or increase the horizontal lines of smaller rooms such as bathrooms. One tiling trick is to break up what may become a large monotonous wall of tiling by inserting a line of different sized or coloured tiles.

Unglazed ceramic tiles have a softer effect on an area, not only because they generally come in softer, more natural shades of colours, but also because they don't reflect light as strongly as glazed tiles. They do, however, have to be sealed with an appropriate sealant to stop them from getting dirty and stained. Their overall effect and matt finish often make them the choice of designers.

Mosaic tiles This term generally refers to smaller sized tiles – less than 50 x 50 mm (2 x 2 in) – and again there is a wide selection to choose from. Mosaic tiles can be laid individually to create decorative patterns or in bigger blocks of colour. Often it is their smaller scale that can work well, particularly in smaller areas such as bathroom or kitchen splashbacks. Although they can be relatively cheap to buy – usually sold on 300 x 300 mm (12 x 12 in) mesh sheets – mosaic tiles take longer to fit and grout due to their smaller size and the greater number required. One advantage of using mosaic tiles over larger tiles, however, is that by positioning them carefully in the space you can get away without cutting them – a big plus for the first-time do-it-yourself tiler. As with ceramic tiles, they look great and last for ages, so make a satisfying project.

Quarry tiles These are unglazed, naturally earth-toned tiles, which usually come in browns, reds, terracottas and cream colours. Their mottled, earthy palette will give a rustic feel to your space, but be careful that the darker colours aren't overpowering.

Something different

Don't get trapped into thinking that paint and wall papers are the only wall coverings available – there are many other, more exciting options that you can use. Have fun and be expressive – it will make your home more unique.

Plaster Whilst this is generally seen as a covering material for brick, block work, or plasterboard walls, plaster used as a top finishing layer possesses a beautiful mottled surface colour. If carried out by an experienced plasterer the finish should be smooth to allow you to paint directly onto it, or, if you prefer, you can preserve the surface to complement the room design. It's a good idea to seal the plaster once dry to prevent it from being marked or releasing dust. This can be done using a matt lacquer or just two coats of a watered down PVA glue.

Should you decide to paint the plaster wall, cover it first in a 'wet coat' (a 50/50 mix of water and your chosen paint colour). This is needed as fresh plaster will absorb a large amount of paint on the first coat. Once this is dry, you can continue painting with undiluted paint.

Brick Exposing the natural brickwork of your home has become popular over the last few years, as it expresses the architectural quality of your home and has a warm visual texture. It can be done with a (rented) sand blasting machine but is very messy and should be carried out by professionals Once finished and cleaned, the wall should be painted with a product known as "water seal" or a watered down PVA glue to prevent brick dust.

Wooden boards Tongue-and-groove softwood boards can give a soft natural feel to a space. The vertical lines provide a gentle rhythm without dominating the atmosphere of the room. They also help insulate the interior from cold temperatures and give it a softer, less echoey feel than plain painted walls. Tongue-and-groove boards can be fitted across the entire expanse of a wall or simply halfway up, then topped with a shaped profile piece so as to break up a large expanse and alter the proportions of the area. They will have one protruding edge (the tongue) which will slot neatly into an intruding slot (the groove) on the next board along, and can be held in place with a nail into a batten on the wall in addition to a small line of wood glue between the two adjoining boards. The battens should be fixed to the wall in the opposite direction to that of the tongue and groove.

There are a number of ways of treating the boards. Paint accentuates the lines of the boards, and whites or soft muted tones can give a beautifully simple Quaker-style feel to the area. Boards can also be stained for a warmer richer feel, or you could try scorching them with a mini blowtorch – a job best done outside! This brings out the grain of the wood, leaving it dark brown, and enhances the natural quality of even the plainest of boards. Boards that are stained or scorched must be sealed to prevent them absorbing water and stains. They hardwearing quality and durability means tongue-and-groove boards are suitable in rooms such as hallways, bathrooms and many other areas in the home. Wherever you put them, they provide an elegant and stylish look that is relatively easily accomplished by a competent do-it-yourself-er.

Textural wall panels These prevent rooms from looking bland and can be a great way to introduce individuality and a visual focus. The possibilities are endless and sometimes the simplest ideas can be the most effective. For example, multiples of almost anything are visually fascinating to the eye, particularly if there are small variations in each one – think of pine cones or pebbles...

Here are just a few ideas for textural panels to get you started. Remember to have fun with the project!

▶ **Leather or felt squares** Cut squares out of scraps of different coloured leather or felt and staple them to a dark painted backing board. Overlap them like tiles on a roof to ensure the backing board is completely covered.

▶ **Mini sticky memo notes** Glue hundreds of these little sticky notes (white or pastel shades work particularly well) to a painted backing board. Again, overlap them and allow them to curl slightly to increase the feel of texture. Don't rely on their own glue to be permanent – use a water-based paper adhesive.

▶ **Squares of stained plywood** Ask a local timber merchant to cut you a number of 5 mm (¼ in) thick plywood squares – 200 x 200 mm (8 x 8 in) or smaller – and stain or scorch them using a mini blowtorch to bring out the grain. Fix them to the wall with the grain running either in the same direction or at right angles to its neighbours, similar to a chess board, to give a rich warm feel to the room.

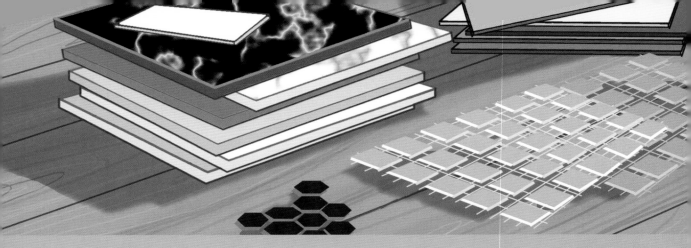

Choosing the right flooring for your home spaces can be a time-consuming and expensive task. Not only do you have to find a floor that falls within your budget, but one that is right for the activity and style of each room. A timber floor may be right for a hallway, where it will take a lot of wear and tear, but may feel bare in a bedroom, where a thick wool carpet may be more luxurious.

Flooring is one of the tools used to help create the right mood and atmosphere. It enables you to make noticeable changes to a room, not only at a junction where two types of flooring meet, but also in the way it feels, and the effect it can have on the acoustics. For instance, you may walk from a lounge carpeted with a thick-pile rug suggesting warmth, luxury and relaxation, through the hallway with a stained and sealed timber floor that reflects light and takes the knocks of family life, to the kitchen, where the stone-tiled floor provides the crisp air of activity and natural beauty.

Flooring

Floors can add character to a space and can be layered with rugs and carpets to add depth and warmth to a room.

Flooring choices

Flooring choices Flooring should always be considered at the mood board planning stage, because it is an essential part of the look of an area, and is likely to take up a large chunk of your budget.

The first thing you need to think about when choosing flooring is the activity that will take place in the room. Here is a list of questions that you might ask yourself:

▶ Will the floor receive a lot of foot traffic, as in a hallway, or less so, as in a bedroom?
▶ Is it likely to get easily dirty?
▶ Will excess moisture be an issue, as in the bathroom?
▶ Do you want the surface to feel warm or cool underfoot?
▶ Will you wear shoes or mostly go barefoot on the floor?
▶ Do you want the room to sound alive and roomy, or soft and cosy?

For every type of room there are likely to be several appropriate flooring options to be considered. These will be differentiated by a number of factors such as purchase cost, laying cost, speed and ease of laying (if it's a do-it-yourself project), durability and function. The main characteristics of various types of flooring are outlined on the following pages; after that, it's up to you.

Laminate flooring

Cost: low to medium **Laying:** easy to semi-skilled **Maintenance:** easy

Photo-effect laminate flooring basically comprises a thick layer of MDF (medium-density fibreboard) with a paper-thin 'photo' of a natural wood floor laminated or glued on top. It is then coated with a thick protective plastic coating. This flooring is widely available and among the cheapest options around, although prices do vary with the quality. Laminates mostly have images of blonde woods and the pattern repeat can be quite small, adding to the artificiality of the end effect. They are easy to lay – comprising snap-together tongue-and-groove lengths – but need to be finished properly around the edges of the room where the boards meet the walls, either by taking them beneath the skirting board or by fitting a thin strip of wood or cork around the perimeter.

Bear in mind that the MDF backing has a lot of formaldehyde glue within it, which can be bad for your health and may cause allergies. In addition, the visual quality of photo-effect flooring decreases with age and it can end up looking bland due to the regular light surface pattern texture. Do note that MDF-backed flooring may be used in most areas of the home but never in rooms such as bathrooms and kitchens, where it may come into direct contact with water, as it will swell, buckle and be ruined.

Engineered flooring

Cost: medium **Laying:** easy to semi-skilled
Maintenance: easy

Engineered flooring is the more natural, higher-quality cousin to photo-effect flooring, comprising of thin strips, approximately 5 mm (¼ in) thick, of prefinished hard wood glued to a softwood backing board. The flooring possesses a natural quality, thanks to the real wood grain, so is considered a good buy. In addition, if the boards are damaged by heels or furniture they can be sanded down a little and

revarnished. They come in a wider selection of colours and styles than photo-effect laminates and reflect the choices possible with a solid wood floor. Although they cost a little more than photo-effect laminates, they are cheaper than solid wood flooring yet have the same beautiful warm effect. The boards are relatively easy to lay, being generally of a tongue-and-groove system. Again, the edges need to be finished carefully but the flooring will not need any maintenance once laid. Check when purchasing engineered flooring whether it can be laid in areas where it may be exposed to water as the laminate glue may not be waterproof.

Solid wood flooring

Cost: medium to high **Laying:** medium to skilled
Maintenance: needs regular maintenance

Solid timber boards tend to be the most expensive of the wooden flooring options although prices do vary depending on the wood type. They come in a vast selection of types and colours, and its warmth and beauty brings a sense of natural charm to homes.

Being a natural product, variations in the colour and grain of the wood do occur, but this is all part of their attraction. One of their downsides is that they expand and shrink with changes in air moisture, so you need to store the boards horizontally in the room in which they are to be laid for ten days before laying so they can adjust. Once laid, if they are exposed to excess water from, say, a burst pipe, they may swell and buckle and never return to their original form. But providing they are sealed properly, they can be used in areas where they will experience a little surface water.

Solid wood floors can be separated into two types: hardwoods such as oak and softwoods like pine. Softwoods are generally cheaper as they grow faster but they are less resilient to damage; hardwoods are more costly but much tougher in resisting dents and scratches. However, if you are on a budget you may want to go for a cheaper softwood, allow it to age a little more rapidly and enjoy that quality.

If you are buying solid wood it is essential that you know that it has come from a reputable source and is not an endangered wood cut from overexploited rain forests. Contact Friends of the Earth or the Forest Stewardship Council (FSC), an internationally recognised organisation set up in California in 1990, who recognize, monitor and stamp sustainable timbers at their source.

Fitting wood flooring When fitting wood flooring, make sure you know the position of any existing pipes or electrical cables – it is an easy and costly mistake to put a nail through a board and into a pipe! Depending on the type of flooring you have chosen – boards, tongue-and-groove planks or parquet squares – you will need to prepare the base floor. This could entail a smooth concrete screed for parquet, or, for planks or tongue-and-groove strips, wooden battens or a proprietary chipboard to nail into or glue onto. Before you start laying flooring, first determine the centre of the room and draw bisecting lines across the area to mark the central point. This way you can lay the flooring from the middle out towards the walls as these may not be truly parallel and are therefore not a good starting point.

Floorboards If you are lucky enough to have floorboards in your home you can use them to bring out the quality and history of the building. They may appear aged and paint splattered but you can easily tidy them up. Start by knocking in any nails that stick out and remove any other protrusions. Then clean the floors by washing them and removing any additional glue or debris with a scraper and pliers. You can now strip them back using a sander – hiring a heavy-duty one is the best option as it will be quicker and more powerful than any sander that you have at home. This is tough dusty work and not for the faint hearted, so make sure you wear the right protective wear (i.e. a dust mask, gloves and knee pads, ear protectors, tough shoes and goggles), and stop dust from flying around the rest of your home by sealing up the doorways with tape or dust sheets. Make sure you always work in the direction of the grain of the wood and never across it. Finally, you can decide how to finish the boards.

Before sealing the floorboards, you will need to treat the gaps between them with a filler material (this can be as simple as papier mâché made from water-based PVA glue and shredded paper). This will contain draughts and dust from beneath the boards and offer some noise insulation. This last point is one to bear in mind as floorboards transmit noise through the house, which may be a nuisance if people are trying to sleep below.

You can finish floorboards in a number of ways to suit the style of the room – these include wax, oil, varnish, stain, bleach or paint (see box, page 76).

Finishes for floorboards

- **Waxes and oils** These are a natural way to treat floorboards but they need to be reapplied every three months. Waxes and oils give the floor a soft natural shine and protect it from water and dirt.

- **Varnish** There are a number of varnishes on the market to choose from, but ideally you will need at least three coats of a product as tough as polyurethane, which comes in matt, semi- or high-gloss finish.

- **Wood stain** Staining is a great way to add character to bland-coloured floors and there are a variety of colours to choose from. A dark wood stain can be a good way to make a cheap pine floor look richer and more luxurious. The stain will only colour the flooring, however, and it will still need to be sealed with a wax, oil or varnish to protect it.

- **Bleach** If you are after a pale wood floor or want to bounce more light into the room, apply a lime wash or light bleach, available from most do-it-yourself or hardware stores. Again, this treatment will need to be sealed afterwards to keep the floor free from dirt and staining.

- **Paint** Natural floorboards, particularly if they are a little scruffy, can look great painted in colours to match the rest of the room. Paint brings out the imperfections of the wood and gives a romantic shabby chic feel. Ideally you should use a proper floor paint, which has resins that make it more durable, and can be coloured to match. Apply at least two coats to cover the floor properly. You could also consider stencilling or painting patterns such as squares on the floor for decorative effect.

Plywood

Cost: low **Laying:** easy to semi-skilled
Maintenance: easy

If you have poor-quality floorboards or a dull chipboard floor that needs covering, you may want a cheap alternative to expensive flooring. Consider using plywood sheet cut into squares of 300 x 300 mm (12 x 12 in). It dents easily but is a quick, cheap and easy do-it-yourself flooring solution, which can look great, particularly when stained. Ask a local timber supplier to cut the squares accurately for you, or even to produce them with a tongue-and-groove-edging. You can then stain, seal and lay them directly onto your floor, playing with the design if you like by laying the grain of adjoining 'tiles' at right angles to one another.

Cork

Cost: low **Laying:** easy **Maintenance:** easy

Easy to cut and finish, cork is another great, cheap and effective flooring solution. Better still, it is completely environmentally friendly as it comes from a sustainable source. You may associate cork flooring with 1970s décor but don't dismiss it. Buy it unsealed and treat it with a dark floor stain before laying for an up-to-date contemporary look. Cork is a great insulator and therefore effective if you have a concrete surface to cover. Ensure your floor is smooth, dry and level before laying the cork, using an approved adhesive and a serrated spreader to give an even layer of glue across the floor. Once the flooring is laid, seal it with several layers of a recommended varnish.

Linoleum

Cost: low to high **Laying:** easy to semi-skilled **Maintenance:** easy

This tough, flexible type of flooring is available in a massive variety of styles and colours. A composite flooring, it is made out of various natural materials, such as linseed, cork and wood, laid on a hessian backing so it is good for people who suffer from allergies or who want a floor made from natural products. It is easy to maintain and needs no finishing once laid in sheet or tile form.

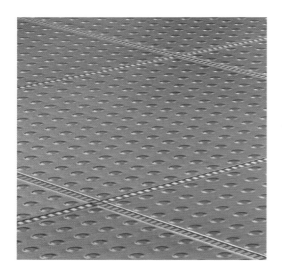

Vinyl

Cost: low to high **Laying:** easy to semi-skilled
Maintenance: easy

The contemporary artificial equivalent to linoleum, vinyl comes in an unrivalled selection of colours and surface patterns, many mimicking other types of flooring such as wood, tiles or metal decking. Prices and styles vary massively and some vinyls cost the same as a solid wood floor. Although largely affordable and warm underfoot, vinyl has an artificial feel that can seem quite plasticky, so it is not an option for all you nature lovers! However, it is convenient and very easy to lay – with a limited range of styles being sold as tiles or in rolls with adhesive backings. Vinyl should be laid onto a smooth level surface as any protrusions will cause it to split and attract a build-up of dirt. It may be necessary to lay a thin screed of concrete or a sheet of plywood or chipboard as a base. Durable and easy to maintain, vinyl is an effective solution for a variety of hardwearing areas such as kitchens, bathrooms and hallways.

Rubber

Cost: low to medium **Laying:** easy to semi-skilled **Maintenance:** easy

Rubber is a very tough, easy-to-maintain and durable solution to flooring areas – particularly in hardwearing situations such as bathrooms, kitchens and hallways – which will give a funky, colourful and contemporary feel to your home. The more expensive varieties now come in almost any colour you wish to

specify, although there is also a good selection of colours in the cheaper styles. Rubber flooring also comes in a variety of surface textures, which can provide added grip although the deeper textures tend to collect the dirt. Unpatterned rubber flooring in particular has a tendency to show up dirt and so needs regular cleaning.

Laying rubber flooring can be a simple do-it-yourself project as it comes in either sheet form on a roll or as interlocking squares so it is easy to work with, but must be laid on a smooth, dry surface. If you are laying it on concrete it may be a good idea to put down a smooth latex or concrete screed, or a layer of plywood or chipboard as a base.

An alternative to rubber sheet or tiles is to have an industrial-style rubber floor poured into your area. This must be carried out by professionals, but the advantage is that it has a smooth seamless finish, which is great for bathrooms and kitchens.

Metal decking

Cost: medium **Laying:** skilled

Maintenance: easy

Once the preserve of industrial flooring, decking in stainless steel, aluminium or galvanized steel has become more popular for domestic use in recent years. The material has the advantages of being very hardwearing, waterproof and non-slip due to its surface texture. It is, however, very difficult to work with, as it requires careful cutting before the seams are fitted and welded afterwards. In addition, you need a solid fixing to work from, such as base sheets of plywood or chipboard, to prevent the decking from sounding thin and tinny. It is an expensive option and if the industrial look is what you are after, you may do better to find a steel decking-style vinyl tile, which won't be as hardwearing but easier and cheaper to work with and without the hard textural or acoustic feel created by metal.

Concrete

Cost: low to medium (if completed by professionals) **Laying:** easy to semi-skilled

Maintenance: easy

Concrete has earned itself a bad reputation over the years but many designers are starting to appreciate it for its soft, muted grey-brown tones and versatility. As flooring, it is cheap, easy to experiment with and produces a seamless slab-style floor that is very tough. However, it is heavy and inappropriate for anywhere other than an existing solid floor on a ground floor or basement.

If you want to keep the concrete finish, but want it to be smoother, you can rent a trolley-like concrete grinder to remove any bumps or ridges, then clean it up using a rotating disc polisher and an appropriate polish that the hire shop should be able to supply you with.

Alternatively, you could use a basic levelling compound or latex screed (available from any building supply centre) that, when mixed with water, pours like a liquid and will create a smooth level concrete grey surface. This will then need to dry or 'cure' for at least two days bvefore it can be painted or sealed. Concrete floors can either be painted with special, resin-based, tough, floor paints that come in a limited range of colours, or protected with a polyurethane floor varnish or lacquer, to allow them to resist marks and scuffs but retain their natural colour. In either case, at least two coats should be applied to resist wear.

Stone tiles

Cost: high **Laying:** skilled

Maintenance: easy

Stone floor tiles provide a beautiful, natural and unique textural surface that will last for years. They are, however, extremely expensive and as costly to lay as they are to buy, so if you are on a tight budget you would do better to look at the ceramic tile section for look-a-like tiles. Stone floor tiles come in a variety of different types, such as marble, limestone or slate, and finishes like polished, honed (a matt finish) or rippled for a more rustic feel. Although cold to the touch, the tiles can be combined with an electric or hot water underfloor heating system for a beautifully warm inviting floor.

Due to the cost of natural stone tiles and the difficulty in cutting them accurately, it is advisable to pay a professional to lay them. They need to be laid on a smooth flat surface – for example, freshly laid screed or a board such as plywood. Bear in mind that grout attracts dirt so it is better to use an off-white grout that complements the tiles; darker grouts will give your space a pronounced grid effect.

Floor tiles

Cost: medium to high **Laying:** skilled
Maintenance: easy
You have only to visit your local do-it-yourself or tile store to see the vast range of styles, colours and prices of floor tiles available. They are hardwearing and long-lasting but also tough if you are clumsy – anything delicate that is dropped on them will smash spectacularly!

There are several basic types of floor tile to look out for:

▶ Ceramic tiles – these are very durable and have a highly-finished glazed quality with clear-cut edges.

▶ Quarry tiles – these are more rustic, naturally coloured tiles.

▶ Terracotta tiles – these are made of natural clay and fired in a kiln, and can often feel warm to the touch.

▶ Unglazed tiles – these have a matt appearance and need sealing and maintaining with linseed oil and wax.

Floor tiles are also difficult to cut and lay yourself, so it may be best to hire an experienced professional, the cost of whom should not be forgotten when buying the tiles. The tiles need to be laid on a smooth, flat surface to stop them from cracking or raising.

Mosaic tiles and irregulars Mosaics refer both to smaller-sized conventional tiles and to fragments of broken tile that have been laid and grouted together.

Mosaic tiles come in a variety of styles and colours and can look great as a floorcovering, resulting in an intense grid pattern, where the overall effect blends together. The tiles can be used in images and abstract patterns to great effect, seen historically in a number of Roman palaces but also used increasingly by contemporary mosaic artists and designers. Mosaics look wonderful but are a real labour of love and can take weeks to complete, generally being laid out in sheet form in a studio and not laid piece by piece on-site.

Fragment mosaics, as used by the Spanish architect Antoni Gaudi in many of his schemes, can look wonderful and give a unique quality to the surface being covered. While it can be a wonderfully satisfying and pleasing do-it-yourself project to take on, mosaic work will take its toll on both your hands and your patience and is almost certain to take longer than you expect to complete. It is a good idea to try out your ideas on a small panel first before commencing a whole floor to get a feel for the mosaic's look, the grout colour and the time it takes to complete.

Carpets

Cost: medium to high **Laying:** easy to semi-skilled **Maintenance:** regular vacuuming and occasional washing

Carpets are regarded as the ultimate in luxury furnishings. Soft underfoot and comfortable enough to lounge around on, they give your home a wonderful sense of cosiness. But from a stylistic point of view, gone are the days of fitting wall-to-wall carpet. They trap dust, are difficult to clean, expensive to buy and fit, and really last only around seven to ten years. Instead, carpet should be seen as a material that can add luxury and comfort to certain rooms such as bedrooms and practicality to areas like stairs where they can reduce noise.

But in other locations – for example, bathrooms, dining rooms and toilets, carpeting is now thought to be inappropriate as it tends to hold stains and smells. Think of it as a means of adding to the effect of a room – a tool to suggest relaxation, comfort and warmth. You can also use carpet as a way of zoning space in order to suggest comfort in one area, while the use of a harder-wearing type of flooring in another area denotes its different function.

Types of carpet Traditionally, pure wool carpets were the only option for a quality carpet and commanded a high price, but manufacturers have now experimented with a variety of other materials such as nylon, polypropylene, acrylic and polyester – on their own and as a percentage mix with wool – to produce durable and static-free cheaper carpets. The quality of these is such that it is now difficult for the untrained eye to tell the difference. One of the

Natural fibre carpets

▶ **Coir** This is the most hardwearing of natural fibre carpets. Its toughness makes it appropriate for heavy foot traffic areas such as stairs and hallways. It has a latex backing, which increases its strength and prevents dust from penetrating from the floor beneath it. When first purchased, it should be left for 48 hours to acclimatize (shrink or expand) to the humidity levels in your home before being laid out.

▶ **Sisal** A more expensive option than coir, sisal comes in a larger range of surface textures and patterns. It can be made into carpets or rugs and, although generally a light brown colour it can also be dyed. Sisal should also be left to acclimatize before being fitted.

▶ **Seagrass** This tough, stain-resistant option is well priced in relation to the others. It is soft underfoot and again, should be left to acclimatize for some time before being fitted.

▶ **Jute** This is the least hardwearing of the four, but also relatively cheap. It should be treated more carefully and placed in areas of less hardwearing foot traffic.

tell-tale differences is a carpet's reaction to excess heat – where wool will smoulder, synthetics tend to melt or burn, leaving holes that are difficult to deal with.

In addition to wool carpets, there are a selection of other natural fibre materials such as seagrass, jute, coir and sisal, all of which can add a sense of contemporary style and a warmth to your home equal to that of the traditional carpet. Although they may, at first glance, appear similar, the selection of natural fibre carpets have different characteristics (see box, page 83).

When buying carpet, tell the retailer where you intend to lay it as this will give them an indication of the level of wear, known as the durability rating, that it will receive. If a classification system is not displayed on the carpet, ask the retailer.

Types of carpet pile The pile of a carpet is as important as the type of fibres. Carpets are either woven or tufted. With a woven pile, the fibres of the carpet are interwoven in a grid formation into the foundation material, which has the appearance of a loose mesh. But with a tufted carpet, the fibres are simply pushed through this mesh and then glued to an adhesive backing to hold them in position. With both types of pile the fibres can be treated in a number of ways in order to create different effects in the carpet.

▶ Cord pile – as the name suggests, the fibres are pulled tight against the foundation material to create a tight, cord-like appearance.

▶ Cut pile – the loops of the material are cut so that the fibre ends are exposed, giving a velvet-like feel to the carpet.

▶ Looped pile – the fibres are looped over and the pile length can be short or long.

▶ Shag pile – the fibres are between 25 and 50 mm (1–2 in) long – a rich luxurious length suitable only for low-use areas.

▶ Twisted pile – the looped pile is twisted and fixed back into the foundation. It has a coarse texture and is appropriate for areas of hard wear, such as hallways and stairs.

Underlay A carpet will benefit from the addition of a good-quality underlay in three ways. Firstly, it will prevent dust from rising through to the carpet from the floorboards beneath and will stop the lines of the floorboards showing after a time. Secondly, it will cushion the carpet, making it softer to walk and sit on, and gives it a richer, more luxurious feel. Thirdly, it will lengthen the life of the carpet as it will take protect it from rubbing directly against the boards beneath.

Underlay is made of either thick felt or textured rubber. Theoretically, a foam- or rubber-backed carpet does not need additional underlay but it will benefit from it anyway.

Carpet tiles These come in a wide selection of piles, colours and styles. Although they are traditionally seen in commercial spaces, the range of designs are now good enough to put in your home. You can lay plain banks of colour or mix up selections of primary colours for a funky, bold, graphic look. Easy to cut, fit and lay yourself, tiles make a satisfying do-it-yourself flooring project.

Rugs These are great way to combine the ease of use of a solid floor with the comfort of a soft, warm surface on which to relax. Rugs also provide the opportunity to add colour and visual texture to a room that may otherwise lack a focus. In a lounge, the addition of a rug in front of a sofa gives the seating area a sense of warmth and luxuriousness, allowing people to sit on either surface. Similarly, a wooden-floored bedroom can benefit from the sensual

quality of a rug placed beneath the bed to step onto when getting in or out of bed.

Despite the wide range of rugs available, they can often be an expensive option. A good idea for a simpler look is to choose a carpet that you like and pay the retailer a small fee to have a piece whip-stitched to the correct size for your room. This is when the edges are stitched in the same thread colour to prevent fraying, giving you a plain, custom-made rug for a fraction of the cost of a purpose-made one.

TIP: Bear in mind when buying flooring that there are often additional costs that bump up the overall price – it is rarely just the cost of the floor that you should factor into your budget. For example, you may need underlay for a carpet or a layer of chipboard to go beneath tiles, or even a protective finish such as a sealant or varnish. Always find out about such additional elements by asking what the floor needs to be laid on, and how it should be fitted and finished.

This may seem a dull subject but considering how to incorporate adequate storage within your home should really be one of your first considerations when moving into and planning a new home. If you are looking to make over and reorganize your home it's likely that good storage is one thing that you don't have enough of and should really focus on. Concentrating on this aspect early on in the thought process of a project will allow you to make the best use of the available space, as opposed to trying to squeeze it in later on.

Let's face it, we live in a consumer society. We buy things we need, things we like – and we are sometimes given things that we don't like (and have to hide them till that person comes round to visit and it miraculously reappears as the centrepiece again!). Whatever the means and reasons for acquiring possessions we all have objects that we keep around us. The problem is that these objects easily become clutter and, in my view, a cluttered home means a cluttered mind.

Storage

Dealing with clutter

Deciding what is and isn't clutter is very much a personal choice. What you choose to leave on show will demonstrate to others what is important to you in your life – be it artwork, collections of natural objects, books, CDs, ornaments, heirlooms, flowers or even your collection of beautifully hand-crafted china puppies! Good storage does not necessarily entail a blank wall of cupboards but also offers you the opportunity to display items.

The choice of what you store and what you display is up to you, but it's useful to regularly take a fresh look at your home and decide whether clutter has managed to creep back into your life. This goes for each of the rooms in the house – and you must learn to be ruthless about what stays and what goes.

Sentimentality only allows your home to become a depot for objects that have no other place to go.

Remember the words of the great Victorian craftsman and poet, William Morris: 'Have nothing in your houses that you do not know to be useful, or believe to be beautiful.'

Good storage...

► Allows you to circulate around the home without tripping or knocking objects over

► Lets you centre yourself and reduce 'clumsiness'

► Allows you to focus on leading your daily life rather than living with the collections of your life

► Reduces visual clutter, allowing the important items in your home to shine out

► Allows you to access whatever you need quickly and easily

► Reduces the amount of dust, making your home easier (and faster!) to clean

Types of storage

Types of storage As a rule, each room in the house needs 10–15 per cent of the total floor area dedicated to storage for the rest of the space to be clear and free of clutter. Storage needs to be thought about in two ways – 'daily storage' for everyday objects and 'deep storage' for items that you need only occasionally. Daily storage should be convenient to reach in terms of height and ease of access, while deep storage can afford to be slightly less accessible. Storage is explored later on in relation to each room in the home but there are a number of ways to tackle your storage issues, so do explore all the options.

As it is unlikely that you will have the luxury of dedicated storage rooms in your house it is worth being open minded and inventive when thinking about storage opportunities in your home:

▶ Look for areas beyond the main circulation routes of your home, for example behind doors or either side of windows. You could even make use of unused space above head height.

▶ Look for classic storage areas and make the best use of them, for example under the stairs, above existing cupboards and in the attic.

▶ Consider built-in furniture such as window seats or platforms, which can offer clever storage beneath.

▶ Look for unused areas in hallways that could store books or coats.

When deciding on what storage needs to go where, you will almost certainly find it useful to take a fresh look at your home and see which objects have been left lying about. Are there specific items that are producing a cluttered feeling? Where would you look to store them in the immediate vicinity if you were to keep them close to hand? Take note of naturally forming piles of objects like books and magazines as they are great indicators of how you live your life and what your needs are. They also show you what items really need to go where. The concept of finding storage space for an item in the area where you actually use it is an obvious but good idea that will make your life much easier and more efficient.

Storage options

Choosing the type of storage you are after is determined by whether you wish to conceal or display what is being stored, and whether you wish the storage item itself to become a feature in the room, or to simply disappear. Every room will need some storage element, so think carefully about it – do you want functional distinctive pieces around you, or a sleek and minimal look?

Your main choices when it comes to storage are:

Built-in A one-off storage unit that makes maximum use of an otherwise underused space – for example, a storage seat, a hallway cupboard or floor-to-ceiling wardrobes in the bedroom. Bedroom wardrobes can be filled with a number of useful elements to make them more functional, such as sliding drawers, rails and shelves. These can be purchased from most good furniture and DIY stores, and inserted into the design of your built-in unit.

Freestanding Buy a new item with specific storage in mind, such as a bookcase, sideboard or wardrobe. Alternatively, an antique or second-hand piece would add character to your home, and you could think about using a second-hand item as the basis of a do-it-yourself project that you could paint, cover in fabric, print images onto, stick objects on, add graphic text to, wallpaper, or even light using rope or fairy lights.

Flat-pack Available from do-it-yourself stores and mail-order catalogues, flat-packed storage items are cheap and convenient but rarely the ultimate choice in style or efficiency.

Fabric and hanging units These come in a variety of shapes and sizes to store shoes and clothes. They are best used in conjunction with a hanging rail, or a secure hook from the wall or ceiling.

Shelving This includes open shelving, metal brackets, spine and bracket systems, shelving fitted into an alcove, floating shelves (with no visible fixings and good for display), freestanding shelving units and hanging shelves (which use a system of wires to suspend shelving from the ceiling).

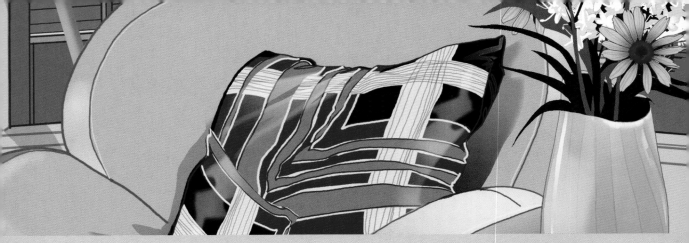

One of the final aspects to consider is the styling of your rooms, using furniture, fabrics, soft furnishings and assorted objects. This aspect of interior design allows you to add an additional sense of layering to your space, which can add comfort, colour and character to your home and allows you to bring areas to life through the careful choice of the objects you choose to have within them. The trick is not to overclutter areas and to provide the objects you do want in your home with enough space to look special and meaningful in their own right.

While a freshly decorated and newly furnished room can be exciting, it can look bland and characterless if everything is new, so try and find ways of mixing old and new elements to give your room character and texture. For instance, you could add a new floor rug to a stripped and polished existing wooden floor and team a worn, leather sofa with new cushions and throws. Combining textured patterns and materials in this way will also give the room some layered interest.

Furniture and finishing touches

Using pattern and visual texture

Much of what you add to your home in the form of final touches will provide visual texture and add a layering of pattern. From an early age the human eye seeks out pattern and texture to stimulate the visual senses, and their addition creates a focus for your space that will draw you in. You can use your décor to express your character and interests, and add vibrancy by including accent colours, fabrics, soft furnishings, plants and flowers.

Patterns can draw your attention to an area or detail, soften the harsh edges of an area and even extend the lines of a space across a wall or up to the ceiling. But you must be careful how you use them. Too many patterns will overcomplicate a space; the right amount will create a sense of intelligent, thoughtful luxury. In addition, patterns can be mixed but you must understand how to do this to make them work together. Patterns are basically one of three basic types, floral, geometric or organic (those that mimic the swirling organic forms of nature), whose shapes repeat obviously or in a more subtle hidden way. To combine different patterns, consider at least one of the following 'rules':

▶ You can mix different patterns if they are from the same genre, be it chintz, geometrics or stripes.

▶ Changes in the scale of the pattern will also work — for example, a large rose head on a single cushion combined with a succession of much smaller ones on another, or a series of wide stripes combined with pinstripes.

▶ Colours also bind patterns — for example, the background colour on one could be the dominant shade on another — this could help you combine light and dark patterns together.

Pattern and texture are largely evident in the fabrics of a room, such as carpets, wall hangings, upholstery, cushions, and curtains. They stimulate your senses and can be fun to experiment with from season to season.

Window dressings

Window dressings One of the key fabric areas of your room will be your window dressing. This will be decided partly by the function of the window – for example, whether it needs to let in light but not prying eyes, and partly by the style and look you are trying to create. There are a variety of ways you can dress your windows – some options, like Venetian blinds, have a harder, more masculine feel, while others give a softer, more romantic look – for example, lengths of long, white cotton. It is important to decide whether your priority is a complete blackout for your space or to prevent heat from escaping through the windows. Fabrics also allow you to soften the acoustics of a room – materials will soak up sounds and reduce the sense of echo.

Curtains These allow you to add an additional fabric layer to the room, and incorporate visual pattern or texture, This can complement or contrast with your colour scheme, depending on the look you want.

When considering purchasing fabric for curtains, make sure you know the width and drop of the window you want to cover. Firstly, decide whether you want your curtains to fall to the sill only or right the way down to the floor. If you have a radiator directly beneath your window, however, you should take your curtains only to sill level and no further. Although floor-length curtains can improve the vertical lines of a room and give a more

luxurious, elegant feel, they do have a tendency to get caught up in furniture, collect dust and prevent heat from the radiator entering the room properly.

Secondly, bear in mind that you will probably need to buy enough fabric to cover twice the width of the window in order to give the curtain a fullness and sense of shape. In addition, you will need to add at least 30 cm (12 in) to the drop of the curtain to allow for sufficient material for turnings at the top and bottom. If you are after a more contemporary-style curtain that is not gathered or pleated, even the most inexperienced seamsperson can create a flat panel of fabric – this could be little more than a flat pillowcase – to simply hang over the window. This can also be a good option if you are working to a very small budget!

Once you've chosen the fabric for your curtains, you also need to think about lining them. Generally, a good-quality curtain is made up of the curtain material itself, an interlining and a lining, which together give your fabric a greater sense of shape and volume, and create a much more professional luxurious look. In addition, a lining stops the sun from bleaching your fabric, helps prevent heat loss through the window and the intrusion of sunlight through your curtains (a special blackout lining is particularly effective for this).

Ideas for personalizing curtains

- ▶ Experiment with stencils and fabric paints to create borders or patterns.
- ▶ Use photo-transfer materials (these are available from art shops) to add pictures of flowers, shells or other favourite images.
- ▶ Sew clear plastic pockets onto plain fabric and fill them with attractive objects like dried leaves.
- ▶ Dye existing curtains an exciting colour to match or contrast with your room. Consult the dye product instructions carefully or contact the dye manufacturer for advice on the right quantity and combinations of dye to make the specific colour you are after.
- ▶ Hem plain curtains with an eye-catching edging like sequins or tasselled fringing.

Although buying the fabric and making your own curtains may be the cheaper option, you could also look at buying ready-made curtains from a variety of high-street stores and fitting them to your windows. This could also provide a great opportunity for you to personalize your curtains as a do-it-yourself project (see box above).

Curtain accessories There are a number of different ways to hang curtains and drapes (particularly heavy curtains). Some provide an additional feature or detail to the window dressing, others are intended to conceal the method of hanging the curtains.

▶ **Track** – made of plastic or metal, this is the traditional way of hanging curtains and relies on a system of hooks that twist into 7.5 cm (3 in) heading tape sewn onto the back of the curtain. This method has a professional overall finish to it. The more expensive systems include a pull cord open-and-close system, incorporated into the track.

Bear in mind that sunlight deteriorates plastic tracks within about four years so replace them once they start to become brittle. Wiping petroleum jelly or a spray-on silicon along the track will prolong the life of curtain track and improve the glide. The advantage of tracking is that it can be wrapped around a bay window or curved wall, allowing you to make the most of your space.

▶ **Poles** – made of wood or metal and available in different thicknesses, poles are best used where the curtains are hung over straight runs, unlike tracks which can bend around corners. They can be used in conjunction with simple rings (pegged onto the fabric or hooked into heading tape), with tab-top headings (where the loops of fabric are slipped directly over the pole) or even with curtain fabric with oversized metal eyes punched into the heading. Offering a contemporary simplicity and relatively easy to use, poles provide a potentially neater detail at the head of the window and can be enhanced by the addition of decorative finials at the ends of the pole.

▶ **Wire cable** – a wire cable system fixed to the walls by metal brackets can be used with curtains that have either metal eyes punched into the fabric or, simplest of all, a series of metal rings with small spring-loaded clips attached to them. Just clip your curtains on to the cable – it couldn't be easier!

▶ **Tie-backs** – these are a means of keeping curtains at the edge of the window to bring the maximum amount of light into a room. Tie-backs could be braided from cords, or made from a scrap of fabric left over from your cushion covers or another fabric element in the room, making a connection between this and your tie-backs. Alternatively, you could keep the tie-backs in the same colour as the curtain for ultimate simplicity.

▶ **Pelmets** – these are the decorative boards found at the head of curtains, often used to hide the messy details of curtain tracks and fixing systems. Pelmets have now largely become stylistically out of date and are seen as a heavy addition to the top of your window that cuts out additional light, creates dark shadows up by the ceiling and attract dust. They are often made of fabric, but could equally be made of MDF (medium-density fibreboard) and painted the same colour as the wall, allowing them to hide the details of your track while blending into the wall surface.

Sheer fabrics If privacy is the only element you need to consider when dressing a window, you may simply want to think about hanging a sheer fabric like voile, muslin or lace, to prevent direct visual access into the room while allowing light to flood in. These thin fabrics are a great, cheap way of dressing windows and can be used as a daytime layer alongside heavier curtains for use at night. This may be necessary as sheer fabric becomes transparent when lit from inside at night. It's worth visiting a few fabric shops or high-street stores to check out the vast range of sheer fabrics available, which come in a number of different colours and qualities to suit every interior space. When considering the quantity you need to buy, purchasing double the width of the window to be covered will provide enough additional fabric for your sheer curtain to hang in a full-bodied, gathered way, although triple width will give a better overall finish.

One of the simplest ways of hanging sheer curtains is to sew a narrow casing at the head of the fabric and then to feed a 'café rod' or curtain wire through it, fixing it to the window frame with hooks at either end. This will allow the fabric to gather neatly along the width of the window.

Because of the flimsiness of the material, don't try to stitch panels of sheer fabric together as the seam will inevitably pull and

These floor to ceiling rouched sheer drapes give the room a sense of elegance that softly filters the natural light, giving the whole room a gentle glow.

rip. You will also have problems when the light is shining through the curtains, as you will be able to see the seam and it will look ugly. Simply sew the panels together at the heading only and allow them to hang down next to one another.

Blinds Blinds offer a number of opportunities to create a neat, stylish finish to a window. When closed, they will cover the window completely, and when open, they will prevent only a minimum amount of light from entering the room. There are a wide variety you can choose from, and all will allow you to control the amount of light entering the room and the desired level of privacy. Generally fixed to the top of a window, fitting blinds is an easy DIY project that can be completed with (generally successful) stylish results!

Roman blinds These consist of horizontally mounted swathes of fabric, and in their simplest form, they can add a sense of elegance and horizontality to your room. Roman blinds can be hand-made or you can buy ready-made ones from a high-street shop. They are easy to fit and to operate and allow you to control the amount of light that filters into your room as you can incrementally raise them and tie them off. Their folded pleats offer simplistic detailing, which is acceptable to both the traditionalist and those interested in contemporary design.

There are a variety of blinds available to suit differing needs and tastes. All will add a sense of clean lined style and practical simplicity to your home.

Venetian blinds These offer great flexibility in controlling the light entering your room, privacy and the atmosphere. They have a simple-to-operate mechanism that allows you to control the vertical height of the blind, raising it or dropping it to the sill, while a separate control mechanism operates the twisting mechanism of the horizontal strips, allowing you to open them fully to bounce light into the room at an angle or to screen out the light completely by keeping the strips closed. Venetian blinds are available in wood, metal or plastic and in a variety of different colours. They come in a range of standard sizes so the chances are that you will be able to buy either one or several to fill a window. If you cannot find one that fits your window frame perfectly, you can buy special cutters to trim the blind, allowing you to cut each strip down to the size required.

Although they provide a strong sense of horizontal lines and easy-to-use flexibility, the disadvantages of Venetian blinds are that they can feel cool and can be a nuisance to clean all those horizontal surfaces that attract dust, often leading them to look dusty and unloved. You can buy a purpose-made simple cleaner, which looks a little like scissors with foam strips for blades, to make cleaning them easier. Alternatively, remove your blind entirely from the window, place in a bath of warm water and wash the strips down with a sponge and shower attachment, leaving the blind to drip dry before rehanging to let the strings dry thoroughly.

Roller blinds These are a cheap, quick and easy-to-fit alternative to Roman blinds. Fixed with a bracket at the top of the window, they have a spring or pulley system to raise and lower them. They have a simple, contemporary look and come in a range of colours and patterns, although you could decorate a plain one using fabric paints or even photographic transfer film (available from craft or art shops) for a more personal look.

In rooms requiring privacy where you still want some natural light, such as in a ground-floor front room overlooking a street, or in a bathroom, you could use a sill-mounted roller blind. This is operated by a simple system of strings and pulleys, which pull the blind upwards, obscuring the view at a lower level but allowing light to flood in above.

Cushions

The addition of cushions can really give a strong sense of languor and luxury. They can complete the look for a sofa or chair and allow a floor rug to be an inviting alternative seating area. Cushion covers are both easy to make and cheap to buy, and allow you to alter the look of your room relatively easily. Having a neutral-coloured sofa with a series of cushions, for example, gives you the opportunity to change the accent colour or textures and patterns in the room as often as you like.

Whether you make the space light, fresh and breezy for the summer or warm and inviting for the winter, cushion colours and textures are one of the easiest and most flexible soft furnishings. Be careful not to combine too many different textured patterns in your cushions, floor rugs and curtains, as you run the risk of overcomplicating the visual texture to a point where it becomes messy.

You can also use cushions to increase the options for seating in the room. A foam-filled cube, a large cushion or even a beanbag offer the chance to slouch at leisure across your floor. Although these should never provide all the seating needs for a room, they can give a fun and relaxed alternative that breaks down the formality of sofas and armchairs in your space, making it feel fun, young and energetic.

Additional tables These can include coffee tables for creating a focus in the centre of the room, occasional tables for styling and lighting, nests of tables to fulfil a variety of functions, and even sideboards. Not only can additional tables fulfil functional roles in your room (for example, a coffee table), they are also a great opportunity to add to your space the essential layer of styled objects that allows you to portray your character.

Tables let you break up the volume of your room by adding more vertical elements such as table lights, and by separating pieces of furniture like sofas from walls, allowing them a greater sense of space instead of being squashed up against a wall. These horizontal surfaces also give you the chance to position objects in the middle of your room. This creates the illusion of greater space by giving the eye something central to focus on and then on into the distance of the far end of the room.

Left: Cushions will add a sense of luxury and informality to your home whilst offering the opportunity to add a little pattern and visual texture.

Right: Have some fun with your side tables. These smooth, but crude, cast concrete blocks give the room a rustic, yet urban feel, and also have beautiful, simple colours.

Mirrors

Mirrors These have a variety of different uses within the home and can be used as an architectural tool where necessary. Consider your space and think about where a mirror might perform at least one of several different functions. As well as being useful when dressing and for checking your appearance, mirrors are a great styling tool and can lift a design in a number of ways.

Use mirrors to:

▶ Bounce light from windows into long, deep corridors

▶ In the recesses of a dark room to reflect light from a window through the back of the space

▶ To enliven a dead-end space such as a stair landing by reflecting views and light as you move around

▶ Behind lights or candles to double their luminescent effect

▶ As a styling tool to allow you to see the backs of sculptures or to double the effect of plants and flowers, dramatically increasing their visual effect

In addition, consider hanging a mirror ball near a window that receives direct sunlight. As the sunlight hits it, it can produce a dazzling array of dynamic spots of light across your room, which is quite crazy but fun!

Mirrors near windows and doors will bounce natural light into and across rooms, and views out, at intriguing angles.

Display collections When you're considering the final styling touches for your room, it's a good idea to go back to your mood board (see 'Creating a mood board', page 20–1) to consider where you started and how the final layer of design will add to and enforce the concept idea that you originally intended for the space. What objects will really define the look you're after?

Think carefully for a while about the additional items that you want to display as these objects can really add to the message you are conveying in the look of your room. Look at the spaces you have created as opportunities to add to this story. There may be tables, shelves, windowsills, mantelpieces and even small areas of flooring that would benefit from the addition of a beautifully styled object. Use your concept to help you decide what these could be and consider whether any of the following list could be appropriate for the space you've designed and now wish to finish with your final layer:

▶ **Collections of objects** – these are items of personal interest that suggest your character and an eye for detail. They can be anything from collections of shells to glass vases or teapots, although do be careful what you put these on as shelves have a habit of collapsing under the weight of favourite objects!

In this home, collections of coloured vases displayed on open-plan shelving add character and identity to the room.

▸ **A glass vase** filled with objects such as fresh chillies, fruit, marbles or even fairy lights (see 'Fairy lights', page 50–51).

▸ **Bowls** – hand-crafted bowls in geometric shapes, often in groups of three, offer a sense of form and shape in each piece and in relation to each other.

▸ **Books** – piles of books provide a personal message about the sort of person you are and your interests.

▸ **Artwork** – buy a painting, print, photograph or even a sculpture that displays your personal taste and interest.

▸ **Found natural objects** – sticks, shells, driftwood, seeds, pebbles or crystals all suggest a fascination with the natural world and there is a uniqueness displayed within each piece.

▸ **Bought objects** – choose candlesticks or decorative ornaments and *objets d'art*, or just fun curiosities.

Using collections and multiples will always look good, especially if you remember to keep a sense of humour!

▸ **Decorative glass** – items like decanters can be placed on windowsills to catch sunlight and fragment it into the room.

Collections of objects or multiples are often pleasing to the eye, and objects that are similar but not identical provide a particular visual treat. The important thing is for these objects to be given enough space for them to express their individuality and uniqueness. Piles of objects will produce visual clutter, whereas a gathering can produce rhythm and visual poetry.

Plants and flowers Potted plants can bring vibrancy and life to a variety of areas in your home. Not only do they catch movements of air through the space, adding a sense of dynamism to an otherwise static interior, they also provide a shot of natural green, which is attractive to the eye. Plants also have the ability to process air in the environment, turning carbon dioxide into oxygen, which significantly adds to the general atmosphere of the space and is good for our health.

When shopping for plants, consider buying a variety of sizes, from taller, more architectural plants such as rubber and cheese plants to smaller grasses or even natural herbs that can grow in the light from a kitchen window. Observe the instructions for feeding your plants and position them for the correct light and temperature.

Cut flowers are by far the easiest, most obvious styling tip for any space, bringing colour, scent and vibrancy into your home. They are easy to work with and you can create a striking display that will act as a focus.

Choice of flower arrangements is up to your personal taste. There is such a massive variety for sale that you can experiment with different shapes and colour. Position them either individually for simplicity or into more organized bouquets. Make sure you have a selection of simple vases for single flowers, small, medium or large bouquets. These should be kept scrupulously clean as bacteria cause flowers to wilt more quickly. Alternatively, you can create your own flower holders such as old watering cans, tin cans or rows of bottles – be inventive and have fun with them!

Plants add a sense of vibrancy and life to even the quietest corners of your home.

The
Rooms

Bedrooms

It is most likely to be the bedroom that will provide the focus for your private space within your home and you may wish to keep it that way when friends come to visit. In the early stages of making a house into a home, your bedroom will become a sanctuary. It can be important to make this the first room that you make habitable as it is a space you can retreat to, to get away from the chaos of the rest of your house. Once your home is settled, the bedroom will become a new retreat, not only from the rest of your home and the people in it, but also from the outside world. In effect, it becomes your domestic womb space and as such, it is up to you to decide how much you will allow other people to have a say in what goes on there, and even whether you will allow others to see it.

For me, the bedroom presents exciting opportunities in terms of design because it is one of the few areas, along with the bathroom, where you can design the room with all the body's senses in mind. You can think about how the room looks and sounds, what it smells like, how it feels and occasionally tastes, so that you can make your bedroom into a multi-sensory sanctuary that expresses who you are on a number of different levels.

Planning

Planning When planning your bedroom, it's important to think about the different activities that go on there as these all need to be worked into your final design. Make a list – the activities will probably include sleeping, reading, watching television, dressing, storing clothes and books, possibly working and socializing (of all sorts!).

Start by drawing a plan of your bedroom (see 'Understanding your space', page 13) then allocate space within it for all of the activities on your list. Bear in mind that a bed will take up a large proportion of any room and, ideally, you should allocate 15 per cent of the floor space to storage.

On the whole, the majority of bedrooms are made up of a set of parts that fulfil all these functions, but which you can add to in order to personalize your space. These typically include a bed, bedside tables, seating (perhaps a chaise longue, a chair or even floor cushions), dressing table and chair, a work table (if there is no other space in the house), storage (built-in, freestanding or under the bed) and a mirror.

As discussed earlier (see 'Furniture to scale', pages 15–16), it can be a great help to cut out pieces of paper to scale, which represent the size and shape of each of these pieces of furniture. Then experiment with the pieces, positioning them on the plan of your bedroom in order to consider different possible layouts. Quite often, there are a variety of ways in which a bedroom can be laid out, which will affect both the way the room looks and how you use it. Try to think through each of the options you lay out as carefully as possible by considering the pros and cons before making final decisions about locations and dimensions of pieces of furniture. This will make life easier once you get the furniture into the room and save you making mistakes when purchasing furniture.

Remember at this stage that it is important to try to allow enough space to circulate around the room and the furniture within it. For instance, a bed that allows access from both sides will feel more generous and comfortable than one positioned against a wall.

TIP: It is often helpful to write down on a sheet of paper all the activities that go on in any room, particularly your bedroom, so that you can work them into your design scheme.

Concepts and ideas Remember when designing your bedroom that it is the room that will dramatically affect both the beginning and the end of each day. As such, your bedroom is a dual-function space that needs to operate well for both of these times. In addition, it will be your most private room, so think carefully about what you need to make it a highly personal and ideal sleeping space.

When you wake up in the morning it's important that when you step out of bed the start of your day is as calm as possible. You should then be able to make an easy transition from your bed to the room's first daytime function – getting dressed. Your bedroom needs to be well lit, receive natural daylight and allow you enough space to get dressed without colliding into pieces of furniture.

In contrast, at the end of the day your bedroom may be used for a variety of activities to help you relax and give yourself some space. This may involve altering the mood of the room by using curtains or drapes, soft lighting, textural fabrics and even aromatherapy or music. The chance to retreat from the outside world is an important function for your bedroom and may well create the basis of your conceptual idea for the room.

The opportunity to design your ideal bedroom is exciting. It's a means to explore the private side of who you are within your home. You may want your bedroom to be light and airy, dark and romantic, seductive, ethnically inspired, or simply clean and contemporary. Whatever you choose, you will still need to provide for the same daily activities.

A soft sensual bedroom will make a wonderful retreat from the outside world making the start and end of your day a luxurious pleasure.

Lighting

Lighting For bedrooms, you need to consider three types of lighting – general, task and decorative lighting (see 'Five basic types of lighting', page 37). Remember that it is a dual-function room so you must have strong, clear light by day, which allows you to see the colour combinations of your clothes when dressing, and softer, more relaxing light by night, which can be via task and decorative lighting.

Natural daylight will be your primary source of light by day and will invigorate you when you get up in the mornings. Morning light, however, particularly in the summer, can be disturbing and you may wish to fit blackout blinds in addition to any window dressings that you decide upon. The danger is that with too many layers at your bedroom window you may restrict the amount of light that floods in during the day, so consider tying or fixing back curtains to maximize on your available light (see 'Window dressings', pages 94–9).

General lighting As a rule, you ideally want a good, even spread of light over the whole floor area of the room. This is most easily achieved with recessed halogen spotlights, but could also be via tungsten spotlights fitted onto or into the ceiling. However, providing you have sufficient task lighting to cast a good clear light onto any activity areas, such as where you may be getting dressed or reading, then it

Make the most of natural light, and combine it with good artificial light for evening use. Light here floods through the window and is bounced around the room by the pale walls.

may be sufficient to have a centrally mounted pendant light fitted with a lampshade that conceals the bulb to reduce the level of glare.

Ideally, your general light should be fitted with a dimmer switch so that you can balance the level of lighting with the other lights in the room to create mood and atmosphere.

Task lighting Task lighting helps you to see clearly while carrying out tasks such as reading, getting dressed or getting ready to go out. As a result, you should endeavour to put task lights in the following places:

▸ **By your dressing mirror** – this should be positioned at about shoulder height so that it will light your whole body from the front. If possible, the light given off should be a colour that represents natural daylight, such as comes from a halogen bulb – so you can see the colour combinations you are wearing. It could be a floor-mounted standard lamp or just a clip-on light attached to your mirror.

▸ **Next to your bed** – these can be small bedside lamps with shades or wall-mounted lights that shine unobstructed light onto the area where you may be lying and reading. Pick a light or a good lampshade that won't put too much glare in your eyes.

Note the variety of lighting types in this room – allowing the bedroom to be more functional by day, and more atmospheric at night.

▸ **At a dressing table** – consider how actors and actresses have a row of lights around their dressing table, which give a good even spread of light onto the face for applying make-up, without highlighting any upsetting wrinkles. A table lamp or some type of angle-poise light will suffice if you don't want to go to the expense of lots of wall-mounted lights.

Decorative lighting This is the light you'll have fun with, creating different moods and atmospheres. A soft and gentle glowing light in the room will aid relaxation, for example. Decorative lights can be used in a variety of ways and are a great opportunity to experiment with fairy lights, rope lights, fibreoptics, coloured lightbulbs, candles or simply low-wattage bulbs in a favourite lampshade (see 'Decorative lighting', page 49 for more ideas).

Walls When considering the overall scheme for your bedroom, remember that the colour is not simply limited to the colours you put on the walls but also the other design choices that you make for the room. People often rely on a brilliant white for a feeling of freshness, space and modernity. White surfaces reflect a lot of light, however, which can be dazzling and not always suited to the relaxing concept of a bedroom. Think of colour in a way that would be appropriate for a bedroom, so as to achieve a sense of balance while expressing the concept of the room.

Paint With such an overwhelming range of colours to choose from, it can be very difficult to pick out the colour that is right for a bedroom. Although the majority of people opt for a light and airy feel, it can be an exciting area to experiment with both the light and the colour, enhancing the mood and feel of the room. In general, lighter colours give a cleaner, more spacious and lively feel, while darker colours can make a room feel more intimate, cosy and romantic.

It is important to remember that in a room such as the bedroom, there are many other layers that will affect the overall colour effect of the space. You need to consider the curtains, bedlinen, any floorcoverings and additional pieces of furniture when considering the overall look of the room as, proportionately, these can be higher than in other areas of the house. It may be helpful at this stage to take the colours of your bedlinen as the starting point of your colour selection process as these are more limited than the paint colours on offer. Other factors that will affect how the wall colours appear will be the natural daylight available and the softer, lower lighting levels used at night.

Bear in mind when choosing paint colours for your room that tonal ranges of colour (see 'Colour schemes', pages 25–9) have a softer, gentler, more relaxing affect on a space, providing a soft, visual rhyme that soothes the eye. A complementary colour scheme, on the other hand, which uses colours on opposite sides of the spectrum, will give a more energetic, lively feel to the space – an effect that is less restful and may be more appropriate for other rooms in the house.

THIS PAGE: A gentle tonal scheme is complimented by the use of soft fabrics giving this bedroom a calm romantic feel. RIGHT: Use patterned wall paper to make the bed the focal point of your room.

A final point to remember when painting your bedroom is that certain petrochemical paints emit harmful by-products called VOCs (see 'Quality of life', pages 243–4) as the paint ages, which slowly release toxins. So, for a paint that allows you to wake up feeling healthier, pick one with a low VOC level or choose from the ever-expanding range of organic paints.

Wallpaper Be careful not to fill your bedroom with excessive amounts of visual detail.

Although this might initially seem a good idea, too much visual stimulus when trying to relax at the end of a long day can be tiring on the eyes and the brain. However, using decorative or patterned wallpaper in a specific area, such as on a feature wall, will draw your eye towards an element of the room that you want to accentuate or, alternatively, draw it away from a less desirable feature. A wallpapered feature wall will add texture and interest to the room without being visually overpowering.

Flooring Obviously, you can use any of the wide variety of floor surfaces on the market. However, remember that your feet will be open to more sensual opportunities in the bedroom and it can be worth looking into all the different options available (see 'Flooring', pages 70–85 for more information).

Think about the sensual qualities of your flooring and what you want to step onto first thing in the morning.

Carpet The bedroom is probably one of the few rooms that can justify being wholly carpeted for pure comfort and warmth reasons. However, remember that carpets attract and hold dust, which can add to the problem of allergies, and cheaper carpets can contain substances in their backing that may be toxic (see 'Quality of life', pages 243–4). Although carpets are high maintenance, needing regular hoovering, and will decrease in appearance with age, they add to the luxuriousness of your bedroom retreat.

Natural floorboards If you are lucky enough to have natural wooden floorboards in your bedroom, it can be great to strip them back and varnish or even paint them. Wooden floorboards are warm underfoot and have a natural quality that enhances any room. They have the added benefit of acquiring a patina that will improve with age. If you choose to paint them, make sure that you sand back the top layer of dirt and grime first.

Laminate flooring This is hardwearing and sound insulating for the floors below, and traps much less dust than carpet. However, most laminate flooring has an MDF (medium-density fibreboard) backing, which often contains formaldehyde glue. This may release toxins that can lead to an increase in allergies (see 'Quality of life', pages 243–4). It may

therefore not be appropriate for laying in a space such as a bedroom, where you spend long periods of time.

Stone tiles These can be beautiful, textural and tactile although they are best used in bedrooms in conjunction with underfloor heating and floor rugs as stone floors are often cold to the touch.

Wood-effect vinyls These can be a simple, quick and cheap alternative to laminate floors. Vinyls are hardwearing, easy to clean and come in a wide variety of styles and colours, but they can seem a little too hard and plastic-like for use in bedrooms.

Rugs Used in conjunction with a solid floor such as natural floorboards, rugs are an easy way to create a balance between the functional and luxurious aspects of a bedroom. A rug adds focus to a particular area of the room and is a great way of putting a special luxurious touch to a specific spot. For instance, placing your bed on a large rug allows you to step out onto a soft, warm textural surface in the morning. You may want to consider using a custom-made rug or a whip-stitched carpet (see 'Rugs', page 85).

Storage

It's a really good idea to think carefully about the variety of different items you may want to store in your bedroom, some of which you will need all the time, others only rarely. Once you have written out a list of your things (see box opposite), you can see clearly why storage and clutter management are so important for your space. With this number of objects, you need to think carefully about where to put them and, more importantly, where to find them when required.

Built-in cupboards The main advantage of built-in furniture in any room is that it makes the most efficient use of the space. It allows you to make full use of oddly-shaped rooms and floor-to-ceiling heights. You can decorate the doors so as to hide the cupboards within the décor of the room or you can design the rooms so as to make more of a feature of them. When designing built-in cupboards, remember that you will want to store a variety of elements inside so try to allow for a number of different shelf heights and sufficient hanging space. It's also worth remembering that to store clothes on hangers, you should allow 50 cm (20 in) from the back of the cupboard to the front. You can get custom-made wooden doors for your built-in cupboards or, to be more inventive, you could use sliding fabric doors. Adorn the fronts of the doors with one of the many styles of handles available or, for a slick, minimalist approach, use push-to-open catches.

Freestanding units Freestanding cupboards, dressing tables and chests of drawers allow you to add character to your bedroom and give the flexibility to rearrange it whenever you wish. The furniture could be antique, custom-made or flat-packed and decorated as you like.

Shelving Shelving systems can be cheap and convenient forms of immediate storage and are obviously great for clothing that can be folded, or for books or other possessions. However, shelves collect dust and inevitably become overcrowded with objects and clutter, which can lead to your whole room looking more visually cluttered. If you are after a pure, clean space, you need to think about enclosing them in some way. This could be as simple as hanging a length of fabric in front of your shelving system or could perhaps mean that you need to consider another form of storage.

Hooks Hooks are good for temporary storage but create visual clutter and distort the shape of clothes hung on them unless you use coathangers as well.

Storage boxes For objects that don't need to be accessed on a daily basis, storage boxes are an inexpensive and convenient option. They prevent the objects inside them from spilling out around the room and also protect them from dust. Storage boxes are a great idea for keeping long-term storage items hidden beneath a raised bed but they can also be used in a more decorative way – a number of shops now offer beautifully made and designed boxes to suit every style of décor. Remember, good labelling will mean you don't have to look through every box in a desperate search to locate a specific item.

Fabric storage units Usually collapsible and divided into compartments, fabric storage units are great for making the most of your storage space as they hang from rails and let you store sweaters and shoes. They can give your room a suggestion of the traveller in you, if that's the look you are after.

Items requiring possible bedroom storage space

- ▶ Clothes – summer, winter and occasional
- ▶ Accessories, e.g. ties, handbags, gloves
- ▶ Shoes
- ▶ Out-of season bedding, e.g. heavyweight duvet and blankets
- ▶ Bedlinen and towels
- ▶ Toiletries
- ▶ Electrical items, e.g. hairdryer, trouser press
- ▶ Secret storage place for passports, etc.
- ▶ Personal filing area/confidential papers
- ▶ Treasured possessions
- ▶ Books and magazines
- ▶ Photographs

Furniture With many bedrooms being of limited size, think carefully about the key pieces of furniture for your bedroom. They will need to offer practicality, storage, comfort and style. The focus may well be the bed, but the other pieces will help to create the mood and atmosphere of your bedroom.

Beds As the key piece of furniture in any bedroom, the bed often provides the main visual focus for the room. Historically, this was a four-poster bed and although these can now seem incongruous in contemporary homes, a similar sense of intimacy and warmth can still be achieved by draping fabrics above any bed using fabric poles. If you are going out to buy a new bed, think carefully about what it will say about the intended style of your bedroom and what you really want, and whether it fulfils your needs. In its simplest form, your bed could be a series of pallets on the floor. However, unless you are into rough urban chic, then there are a variety of other alternatives you could go for – from simple flat-packed beds made of pine to steel-framed beds and hand-made one-off specialist beds. Your choice will be determined by your budget, intended style and the dimensions of your bedroom.

Beds can come in a variety of heights, and your choice will depend on the style and needs of your bedroom. You may want to be able to sit on it easily, in which case you will want it to be approximately chair height; you may have a low ceiling, so wish to have a lower 'futon-style' bed to increase the sense of height; or you may have storage needs to fulfil, in which case you may want a base that has drawers or a bed on legs that you can slide storage boxes underneath.

Mattresses It is difficult to put a price on a good night's sleep, but at some point you are going to have to, so knowing what to look for when you buy a new mattress is essential. A good mattress is likely to last you between seven and ten years of constant use, providing you look after it by turning it regularly, so if you consider its initial cost and divide that by the number of nights you could be sleeping on it, the figure would be ridiculously small. The point is that you really want to spend as much as you possibly can on your new bed – it will be one of the most valuable purchases that you make in terms of your comfort, health and wellbeing.

This wall length mirror emphasises the luxurious quality of
the bed and increases the sense of space in the bedroom.

Buying a new mattress can be an amusing but tricky process. When you go along to your mattress retailer you must spend as long as possible testing out any mattress you may be interested in. It can feel quite odd lying on a bed in the middle of a showroom for some time, but try to relax and get in touch with how the mattress makes you feel. You should ideally spend at least 15–20 minutes on any mattress that you might wish to buy!

Types of mattress

- **Latex foam** This moulds itself to your body, alleviating areas of pressure by offering constant support all over. It is also hypoallergenic, anti-microbial, breathable and dust mite resistant. However, this type of mattress can be very costly.
- **Open-coil unit** This is the most readily available type of mattress, and prices vary dramatically. The springs are connected by wires and the whole thing is covered with fabric. This type of mattress comes in a variety of levels of firmness.
- **Pocket-sprung** A pocket-sprung mattress consists of individual springs held in fabric pockets, which are clipped together. Their great level of comfort is derived from the fact that each spring works independently from the others, preventing couples sharing a bed from rolling in towards each other.

It will dramatically cut down the selection process to start with if you know what sort of mattress you like – for example, hard or soft or, if you have back problems, an orthopaedic mattress. There are certain facts to bear in mind when buying a new mattress:

▶ The number of coils (springs) in a mattress dramatically affects the level of support it provides. In general, one with 300 coils gives you less support than one with, say, 700, but depending on the quality, a mattress with 412 springs can also be very good.

▶ The quality of the mattress may be determined by the materials inside and the gauge (or width) of the steel used in the coils affects how much support the mattress gives you. The thinner the gauge, the weaker the support, and vice versa.

▶ The interconnecting wire between the springs affects how all the coils work together and hence the mattress's comfort level – too few and the mattress will lose its shape.

▶ The upholstery on the outside of the mattress affects its basic comfort. For winter and summer temperature comfort levels, some mattresses have more on one side of the mattress than the other. Decide how much material covering you feel you need in order not to feel the shape of the springs through it. Make sure you rotate your mattress regularly in order to allow the fabric covering to aerate, or it will start to sag.

Headboards A headboard can increase the sense of luxury in a bedroom by offering a vertical surface to lean against, rather than the wall. Headboards can be plain or padded – buy one ready-made or make your own using a piece of board, a staple gun, a piece of foam and some fabric that matches or contrasts with your room. It is a means of creating a centrepiece for your bedroom, making your bed the focus of the space.

Bedside tables A bedside table adds weight and, with the addition of a bedside light, focus to the room, providing a surface for both styled and necessary items. Bedside tables are invariably used for books, radios, glasses of water, clocks, bedside lights and occasional storage items. Without them, you'll find small piles of objects on the floor next to your bed just begging to be knocked over, trodden on or stumbled over in the middle of the night.

Although you can go out and buy ready-made tables, you may like to make, create or find something that is perfect for the task. Great bedside tables can be made from sections of railway sleeper, driftwood, wooden fruit boxes, cable reels, old chairs and antique furniture, or simply buy adaptable ready-made furniture to suit the style of your room.

Right: The co-ordination of headboard, side table and soft furnishings suggests an attention to detail in this room.

Additional seating Being able to consider places to sit other than on your bed is a luxury and adds to the idea that you can relax in your room. Find something comfortable – anything from an old leather armchair to a chaise longue or small sofa. Large floor cushions with a soft rug beneath them will also seem inviting. Don't forget, anywhere that you might want to sit and read is a good place to put an additional side light.

Soft furnishings add an additional sense of layering to a room and can dramatically alter both the colour and mood of your bedroom. They allow you to try something a little bit more daring by incorporating colours, patterns and textures that, while you wouldn't want to cover your whole room with them, could work fabulously in small amounts. They can also be replaced on a regular basis without breaking the bank.

Soft furnishings can also add dramatic visual interest to a room that might otherwise appear too spartan. They can have an impact on the mood of the bedroom and the idea that you want to portray. Dark and textured fabrics such as velvet add a dramatic luxurious feel, while lighter pastel shades will keep the room feeling cool and contemporary, but still offer a sense of languorous comfort. Alternatively, use different materials, such as cord, damask, shaggy fabrics, cottons and silks, to keep the room feeling fun and relaxed.

Mirrors for the bedroom

▸ **New mirrors** A new mirror can give good clean reflections suitable for getting dressed and seeing your reflection clearly, but can be cold and too harsh.

▸ **Old mirrors** Finding an old mirror, albeit with a mottled, less uniform surface, in an antique shop or market can be a great way to add character and depth to a room.

▸ **Decorative mirrors** These could be small mirrors used for bouncing light around the room or just for decorative purposes to add to the mood and feel of the space. Mirror balls, strings of small mirrors and mosaic mirror tiles are all possibilities.

▸ **Functional mirrors** A large functional mirror in a bedroom is very useful for getting dressed or getting ready to go out. It should be large enough to carry out its function within the confines of the room and ideally situated next to a light that allows you to see yourself clearly. It could be concealed within a cupboard, positioned above a dressing table or left freestanding for added flexibility.

▸ **Space-enhancing mirrors** These can be used in dead-end spaces such as niches and alcoves or above a mantelpiece to extend the perception of space. They are also useful in areas where light falls — for example, next to windows or an artificial light source in order to reflect it into other areas of the room.

▸ **Mirrored ceiling tiles** If you like this sort of thing... Just make sure you fix them to the ceiling adequately!

Soft furnishings for the bedroom

▸ Bedlinen
▸ Bedspreads
▸ Scatter cushions
▸ Curtains
▸ Throws for furniture
▸ Awnings over bed

Bathrooms

From a financial point of view, a beautiful bathroom will add significant value to your home. However, and more importantly I think, it is a real luxury to have a wonderful bathroom – one that will invigorate you in the morning but also relax and soothe away your troubles in the evening, one that is so great that you will want to hang out there and not just wash and leave. It is a space to wash, relax, carry out daily rituals and experience all the senses – it can be so much more than just the smallest, most functional space in the home.

But don't get carried away! The chances are that your bathroom will have to be highly functional, and you will almost certainly have a budget to work to, so the practical details will have to be thought about. Exact sizes and quantities of materials must be calculated carefully and not under- or overestimated. It may be hard work, but it will be well worth it for a beautiful bathing space.

Planning After the kitchen, the bathroom is the one room that needs the most planning so think carefully about your design. Spend time and thought locating each of the items that will have to go into the room as aesthetics will inevitably take second place to function in the early stages of your bathroom planning. Remember that mistakes made at this stage will be expensive to rectify later on due to the cost of sanitary ware, tiles and labour.

Because quantities and dimensions are so critical it's really useful to draw a plan of your room (see 'Understanding your space', pages 14–17). This will allow you to buy the right size of sanitary ware and to make an informed estimate as to the quantity of flooring material and wall tiles you'll have to buy. Many of the materials intended for bathrooms are so expensive that it is essential that you don't overorder. Equally, try not to skimp as bathroom surfaces take a lot of wear from steam and water and meanness will only cost you more later – the corrosive power of water will eat into everything, particularly if something is not fixed or sealed properly.

Once you have your bathroom planned out, the next critical stage is to ensure your materials will be on-site in time for your contractors. Many bathroom products are so bulky that they inevitably have to be ordered in. Delivery times can vary massively and could delay your schedule if items are not ordered far enough in advance.

In addition to ensuring timely delivery of all your products, you need to be aware of the complicated on-site procedure in fitting them. This involves getting a variety of different tradesmen together at the right time – a plumber, electrician, builder, plasterer and tiler all need to be coordinated for first and second fixings. For example, the electrician needs to install cables into the walls and ceiling, and has to come back later on to fix light switches and fittings once the plasterer has done his work. Similarly, the plumber and tiler will have to coordinate their work. As simple as it sounds, it can become horribly complicated as tradesmen are notoriously unreliable and often have several jobs running at the same time (see 'Employing contractors', pages 234–7 for more information). Getting in one contractor to organize his own tradesmen can simplify the process but the temptation for you to use individual tradesmen at a lower cost is difficult to resist, particularly if you are working within a tight budget, and, let's face it, who isn't? But remember, it is difficult to put a financial cost on stress and relying on the goodwill of friends with bathrooms cannot last forever!

Deciding on the layout In planning terms, it is the drainage from your toilet, bath, shower and basin that will really determine the layout of your bathroom. Very often, once you start to lay out these items, there is really only one possible layout. The toilet has to be positioned first because of its large waste pipe. It will invariably have to be situated near an outside wall and as close as possible to a wide-diameter soil stack (downpipe). Creating a new soil stack can be costly so try to work with what you have, if possible. Once the position of the toilet is decided, you have a little bit more flexibility when it comes to the locations of the bath, shower and basin as these have smaller waste pipes. Although this might seem like a boring way to plan out your dream bathroom, having a few restrictions can often help get things right.

At this stage, it's a good idea to consult a plumber to check that you have the layout right with regards to your drainage, water pipes and water pressure.

In general, positioning your bathroom suite around the perimeter of the room generates the maximum space efficiency in what is often a relatively small room. It also makes for easier pipe work. However, for a more unusual look, baths and basins can be placed away from walls and the pipes run beneath the floor. Again, you must check the necessary fall of the waste water pipes to allow for adequate drainage and the location of floor joists.

Having positioned the major items of your bathroom, it's a good idea to use additional leftover areas for elements such as an airing cupboard and radiator or heated towel rail. In addition, think what you will need where. You should find a way of storing toiletries in a convenient location next to the sink for ease of use – use shelving, a mirrored storage cabinet or even a small-wheeled trolley.

A heated towel rail in the bathroom can be a real luxury, even in summer. There is a wide selection on the market to choose from, but remember that you may want to use the rail independently of the rest of your home's heating system so consider an electrically operated one with its own thermostat. This will need to be fitted to a special electrical socket, so consult an electrician first. For a really

This well organised bathroom has all the key elements arranged around the perimeter and a storage cupboard that has been placed on the wall to save space.

thorough finish, consider getting your plumber to fit a hot water pipe loop through the storage cupboard. This will keep it warm, and dry towels and other damp items.

Lastly, from both a practical and legal point of view, you need to consider the ventilation in your bathroom. This is necessary to prevent a build-up of excess steam and moisture as well as the possible build-up of gases if your bathroom also contains your boiler. Ventilation can come directly from a window – it's a good idea to fit a vent – but it will also be necessary to fit artificial ventilation via a fan. This must extract the correct volume of air per minute (contact your local authority about the legal requirements); it needs to be fitted by a builder and wired in by an electrician. It's a little complicated but essential that you comply with building regulations.

Right: Using combinations of materials will allow even a tight space to have character and identity, but ensure that they will all resist the effects of water.

Things to remember when planning your bathroom:

▶ Make sure you know where the stopcock for your mains water supply is in case of any leaks in your bathroom.

▶ See 'Employing contractors' (pages 234–7) for information on finding tradesmen for installing and repairing your bathroom fixtures.

▶ Bathrooms can often be expensive rooms to completely redesign. For a quick but effective make-over, you may want to leave the bath, shower, basin and toilet as they are and just think about replacing the tiles, bath panel, taps and flooring, or possibly just repaint the walls. You could put this together with new towels, a new bath mat and blind and some plants for a fresh clean feel. These are effective ways of making a dramatic change to a bathroom on a low budget.

▶ If the layout of your bathroom makes it possible, a freestanding bath will appear more luxurious than one positioned along a wall.

▶ Ensure that you incorporate within your room design good access to pipes, fixtures and fittings via removable access panels. This will save you having to destroy the finishes to your bathroom in the event of a leak.

Concepts and ideas

Your bathroom can be really exciting, and so much more than just the smallest, most functional room in the house. It is, in fact, one of the few places of calm, peaceful ritual and connection with the elements within the home, so don't miss the opportunity to make it something special.

The bathroom is one of the few rooms where you are really open to your senses and sight (lighting and colours), sound (water or music), smell (aromatherapy oils, scents and perfumes) and touch (textured surfaces, rough, smooth and water) can all be included. Incorporating elements of your design that affect each of these senses will greatly enrich the experience of your bathroom space.

Try and consider ideas beyond the usual beach or seaside theme (turquoise walls, sea shells and driftwood) and challenge yourself a little further. Come up with alternative ideas and colours that will make you feel good and prepare you for whatever lies ahead when you leave your bathroom for the outside world, whether you need to be invigorated for the day ahead or relaxed after a long stressful one.

Lighting Natural light from windows is always hard to beat, but in the bathroom there is a conflict with privacy requirements. You can resolve this by using some type of window obscuration such as sheer curtains, textured obscure glass, frosted opaque glass, glass etch spray or frosted-glass effect film (see 'Retaining privacy', pages 40–1).

The combination of lights on the floor and walls offer flexibility and practicality to this bathroom. This will make it functional by day and calming by night.

Although these are all means of obscuring the glass itself you could also use one of a variety of blinds. My favourite option is the sill-mounted blind, which pulls up – this allows privacy and obscures views directly in, while allowing you to lie in the bath and stare out at the sky through the top of the window. In general terms, try to obscure your bathroom window as little as possible in order to maximize on the natural light available.

As with any area that contains water you must be very careful with electrical items. Electric lighting in your bathroom is no exception, so while it should look beautiful, it must also be safe. Make sure when buying light fittings that you check with the retailer that they are suitable for use in a bathroom. In addition, you must never fit electric light switches that have to be operated with wet hands – you must always use a light pull with the fitting attached to the ceiling. If you want to operate the main light with a dimmer switch, it must be fitted on the wall outside the bathroom.

General lighting Good general lighting in a bathroom is essential as it can be a hazardous space with slippery surfaces. As ever, there are a variety of lights you could use – downlighters, such as halogens or spotlights, wall-mounted uplighters, or even fluorescent strips, which can be concealed behind mirrors or cabinets (although these give off a relatively greenish light which can be unflattering).

The most recent trend for using halogen downlighters is due to the fact that they give a good, clean, sharp source of light in a similar colour to natural light and can be recessed within the ceiling, which makes them safe and reduces their visual impact into the space. Make sure that instead of regular halogen downlighters, you buy ones with the correct safety rating for use in bathrooms. One problem with halogens is that their harsh downlight creates heavy shadows on the face so they are, on the whole, unflattering highlighting any wrinkles, blemishes and signs of ageing. It is therefore a good idea to think about task lighting where you need it most – at the bathroom mirror.

Task lighting This is best used in areas where specific tasks are carried out. In the case of the bathroom, this is around the bathroom mirror, where you are most likely to shave, apply make-up, cleanse your face and brush your teeth, for example. In its simplest form, task lighting could involve two lights on either side of the bathroom mirror, positioned at eye level. This allows light to fall evenly across both sides of the face and directly onto the skin. There are a number of lights you can buy, some of which are incorporated into bathroom mirrors. Although this may seem an unnecessary extra cost on your bathroom budget, it really will make a difference to the way you use the mirror and the way you will feel when you leave the bathroom.

Decorative lighting For a real treat, think about putting a decorative light in your bathroom that will create atmosphere and a sense of relaxed calm to soothe away your daily stresses. Most simply, this could involve incorporating niches or ledges on the wall for candles, but if you really want to go to town – and believe me it's worth it – you may want to think about incorporating plastic insulated rope lights (made to a safety standard for outside use) or even fibreoptic units with their tips poking through the ceiling. This gives the effect of bathing beneath twinkling starlight – pure magic!

Walls Again, because of the high moisture content and humidity of a bathroom, your wall surfaces must be carefully considered and prepared. Where water will hit the surface directly, it's essential that you protect your walls with a completely water-resistant surface such as tiles, glass, stone or metal panels. Without this, a wall will deteriorate rapidly and will soon need repairing. In other parts of the room, you should still remember that there will be high moisture levels.

Tiled surfaces These can prove costly if you want to tile the entire bathroom – it is a labour-intensive process that includes careful preparation of the walls, tiling and grouting. However, if your walls are uneven, you could consider smaller mosaic tiles, which cover bumpy surfaces more readily. You may also want to consider tiling just the necessary areas around the bath, basin and shower enclosure, or tiling up to a half-line on the wall and painting the rest. If you are going to do the tiling yourself, using smaller tiles such as mosaics is easier as you can position the tiles in a way that involves little or no cutting.

Painted walls When you are choosing paint for the bathroom, remember that the room's high moisture content makes ordinary emulsion crack and age very quickly so be sure to pick a paint type that is resistant to the effects of water, such as an oil-based matt or eggshell finish. For a more professional finish, you can use specially formulated bathroom and kitchen paints that will resist the effects of moisture and frequent temperature change. These will give you a longer lasting, more protective finish to your walls, but they are not, however, resistant to constant water splashing in areas such as beside the bath, shower or basin. These areas should be covered with a more hardwearing surface like tiles.

When it comes to choosing paint colours, blues and turquoises are often an instinctive choice for people wishing their bathroom to have a water theme. However, you should remember that any colour you use on bathroom walls will reflect on the skin – blues can be a cold colour, and will make you look paler, while warmer colours such as browns and oranges make you look healthier, an

These mosaic tiles are hard wearing, look great and can be really easy to fit, even by a novice tiler.

important psychological bonus when leaving the house in the morning.

Timber panelling A great simple option for your bathroom walls can be tongue-and-groove timber panelling. It provides a soft natural look, particularly when you have stained or painted and sealed the wood. It should not be used, however, in areas where it receives a constant soaking, such as around the shower, as, despite the sealing, it will soak up the water and begin to go black which is the first sign of rot.

Flooring

Flooring Bathroom flooring has to fulfil five main requirements: it must be hardwearing, water resistant, non-slip, easy to clean and look good. Whilst this might sound like a long list, there are a variety of floors that are appropriate for bathrooms, and that will prevent water from seeping through into the floor below. These include both glazed and unglazed tiles, stone tiles, vinyl tiles, rubber and linoleum (see 'Flooring', pages 70–85 for more information).

You could also opt for solid wood, although it's best not to use a softwood because if water is allowed to sit on it for any length of time it will start to seep in, swelling and staining it. It's best to use a hardwood, some of which like teak and iroko are self-oiling and naturally repel water. These can be very expensive, however. Even well-sealed woods need annual maintenance under hardwearing conditions.

Floors that you should stay clear of in bathrooms are laminates, engineered floors and anything containing MDF (medium-density fibreboard), which reacts badly to water, swelling immediately. Engineered woods such as chipboards and plywood are generally bonded with a water-based glue and will fail when exposed to water for any length of time, although you can specify marine-grade plywood and exterior-grade MDF, which are more water resistant.

TIP

▶ Consider the weight of your bath and the strength of the floor. Remember that 1 cubic metre (35 cubic feet) of water weighs 1 tonne (1 ton); most baths contain about 0.4 tonne (0.4 ton). If you have doubts about the capacity of your bathroom floor, contact a structural engineer or an experienced builder.

▶ To give stone or tiled floors a warm and inviting feel, fit underfloor heating with specially fitted pipes from your heating system or through an electrical loop (the cheaper option). You can lay this yourself, but it may be better to pay an expert to complete it before covering the system over with expensive tiles and realising that you have a leak, or it doesn't work.

Bathroom storage A surprising number of items have to be stored in your bathroom. You need to consider early on in your planning how you will do this, particularly as many of these items are unsightly and will make your bathroom look cluttered – for example, shampoos, gels and soaps; loofahs/sponges; toys for you or the kids; cosmetics, hair-brushes, toothbrushes and toothpastes; towels, bathrobes and bath mats; first aid kit, medicines and suntan lotions; toilet rolls and cleaning products.

Bathroom storage options

▸ **Shelves** Although shelving is the easiest, cheapest option, it also produces the highest level of visual clutter in your space, as shelves inevitably become crowded with various bathroom products. Try to create a built-in cupboard, if possible, to conceal toiletries from sight.

▸ **Mirror cabinet** A ready-made mirror cabinet with built-in storage is an easy and relatively cheap option to buy.

▸ **Storage trolley** A free-wheeling trolley that can be moved around the bathroom offers plenty of storage space via a series of drawer units – a good option for families, where each person can have a separate drawer.

▸ **Under-basin cabinet** A neat built-in unit can be great for items like towels, but inconvenient for regularly used things such as cosmetics.

▸ **Medicine cabinet** This is a useful one-stop place for all your emergency medicines and bandages.

▸ **Airing cupboard** A built-in airing cupboard giving you access to warm dry towels is a great luxury. It can be used to store other items, too, although the heat and warmth are not appropriate for the storage of things like cosmetics.

Fixtures and fittings

The fixtures and fittings you choose for your bathroom are essential to the style and quality of your bathing experience. With so many different elements to choose for the room it can be surprisingly complicated. For example, many bathroom ranges often won't have all the products you are after which can be tricky since coordination is the key to a cohesive look.

Picking the same colour, styles and materials helps the cohesiveness of a look – particularly in sanitary ware such as baths, sinks and toilets. A white suite provides a classic, timeless look, whereas coloured sanitary ware may be fashionable now but will date and age over time.

Taps When choosing your taps, think about the style of the suite you are choosing them for and be consistent with this style for a coordinated look. For instance, if you have

Baths

- ▶ **Steel enamel** These baths are heavy but solid and their hardwearing, resilient enamel surfaces last for years.
- ▶ **Plastic** These baths are less expensive, but can squeak and stretch when filling, which makes them feel cheaper. Their surfaces can be scratched by abrasive cleaners so treat them carefully.
- ▶ **Resin** These are more solid, robust and expensive than plastic baths, but a good buy as they have a greater sense of quality.
- ▶ **Antique/second-hand** Designs such as the classic roll-top bath are appealing, but do watch out for chipped enamel surfaces, which can lead to corrosion of the bath's metal base and remember that they may well need unusual or out-of-date fittings and pipes with odd sized diameters, which can make them difficult to fit. However, they make up for this in quality and their grand sense of romantic appeal.

chosen an antique-style basin, pick decorative, appropriately styled taps and fittings and likewise choose plainer fittings for a more contemporary style of suite.

Thinking on a larger scale, check whether the range you like can provide you with taps for the rest of your home as well. Coordinating the taps in bathrooms and toilets throughout the house will help to give it a more complete feel.

The taps, fixtures and fittings will add a sense of style and quality to your bathroom so think carefully about the look you are after.

Taps are generally fitted to the surface of the appliance they are servicing, but there are other options. For basins or freestanding baths, the taps could be surface mounted next to the appliance, leaving the lines of the sanitary ware free of visual obstruction. Similarly, you could look into wall-mounted fixtures that pour water directly into the bath or basin through an elongated spout. This will require your plumber to chase the pipes into the wall, then plaster over them before fitting the taps and spout. It will also require a little more care and attention when it comes to tiling as the tiles will have to be cut around the fittings. However, the advantages are that not only is it much easier to clean the bath or basin as dirt cannot get trapped around the fittings but the look is much cleaner visually, making it very much the designer's choice.

Whatever your choice of taps you must make sure that you (or your plumber) can easily access the fittings should a fault, such as a leak from a worn washer, occur. This may mean having an access panel in the side of your bath or ensuring when you purchase the taps that the washers can be easily reached.

There are an enormous number of taps for sale and the real problem is finding the right one for you. Don't feel that you have to buy your taps from the same retailer from whom you purchase your sanitary appliances – it's practical to shop around. Try your local do-it-yourself or bathroom store, but it's also well worth your time carrying out a few searches on the internet for newer, better, more appropriate or cheaper products.

Below: These contemporary taps are simple and elegant.
Below right: Wall mounted sink and taps look really stylish.

Basins With such a variety of basins on the market, you don't have to opt for the traditional-style rounded ceramic basin. Look instead at rectangular, square, glass, chrome, wood, wall-mounted and plinth-mounted basins, all of which could give your bathroom a distinctive and exciting look. Your decision will ultimately be influenced by your style and budget.

Traditionally, basins are fitted to the wall but sit on a pedestal, which supports the weight and adds to the look of the piece. You may prefer to consider a more stylish, surface-mounted basin instead, which sits on top of a plinth or wall-mounted shelf. This style provides plenty of room for cosmetic products and improves the lines of your bathroom. Alternatively, you could buy a basin that fits directly onto or into a cabinet, which will offer you a little storage space beneath the basin while also hiding any unsightly pipes.

Again, taps can be surface mounted on the basin – often there are predesignated holes, which can be punched out to fit the taps either to one side or in the middle of the basin. Alternatively, you can wall mount them for a neater, easier-to-clean and stylish solution.

Toilets The easiest way of improving the look of an old toilet is to buy a new toilet seat. You can choose from wood, plastic, padded or even plastic resin seats filled with a variety of weird objects. If you are going to keep your old toilet but can't bear its unsavoury internal appearance, you could try removing the limescale deposits by using a limescale remover or similar products that are available from most supermarkets or hardware stores. Pour it gently into the bowl, taking care to protect your eyes and skin, and stand back and watch it froth!

If you are going to buy a new toilet, you can opt for the traditional floor-mounted toilet or, for a more contemporary look, a wall-mounted one, which will look neater, be easier to clean around and give the illusion of greater space. This is a standard toilet but without the footplate, so it is supported 5–10 cm (2–4 in) off the floor by its wall brackets, giving an impression of greater space in your bathroom as you can see the floor beneath the pan. This is, however, a more expensive option and you will need to think carefully about the structural fixings for the wall.

A concealed cistern hides messy details and offers the opportunity of a functional shelf, which is always useful in a bathroom.

For the designer look, you could opt for a neater, concealed cistern toilet. This is where the cistern is encased in a box unit, which incorporates a special flush button in its top or front. Access to the cistern for servicing is via a removable panel. Stylistically, this has a much neater appearance than the other options – it gives the bathroom tidy lines and the cistern top cover offers a surface that can be used as a styling feature.

Whatever toilet you decide to buy, make sure it has a dual-flush cistern. This allows you to control the amount of water flushed each time, which will save you money in the long run if you have a metered water supply. It will also help to prevent a needless waste of what will become one of the Earth's most prized resources.

Showers For many people, having a good shower in the bathroom is more important than a bath. It's a quicker, easier and more invigorating washing option in the morning. A shower also has the advantage of being much more environmentally friendly – a standard one uses on average just two-fifths of the water required for a bath. Not only does this save money on your water bill but it will be energy and cost saving too.

A shower normally consists of five main parts – the shower tray, the shower head, the valve or taps, the water-protected wall surround and the screen or curtain.

Shower trays Shower trays are generally made of resin or ceramic, but you can get custom-made stone/stainless steel ones, which generally work out very expensive as you will then need a custom-made screen. Get as large a tray as possible for your bathroom – if not square, then rectangular.

Alternatively, if you have little space, you could have an over-the-bath shower. If you do this, you must tile any surrounding walls that may get wet, seal the edges of the tiled walls and bath and have some type of shower screen to prevent water from spraying across the room. Ensuring water doesn't leak in any way is vital, as it can cause expensive damage.

Shower heads You can buy either a fixed or a movable shower head – the latter is often attached to a flexible hose. Although this style is probably more convenient, it attracts dirt and limescale deposits, and the hose deteriorates over time. There are a surprising number of shower heads on the market, some with adjustable pulse or massage fittings and others with fixed pressure.

Shower taps Go for as minimal a fitting as possible as water flow readily attracts a build-up of dirt and limescale on the fittings. Try not to economize by having surface-mounted pipes as again the water will eventually corrode the pipes and their joints, and look

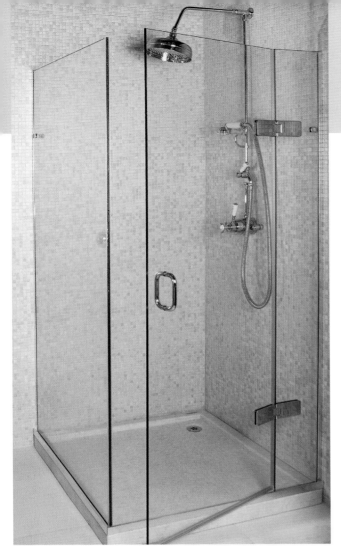

scrappy. It's worth paying for them to be chased into the wall by a plumber and then plastered and tiled over.

Finding suitable shower taps and fittings can be quite a challenge as they vary in price dramatically. If you have a budget in mind, try to stick to it and don't be swayed. If possible, pick a set of shower taps that are 'thermostatically controlled'. This is an in-built valve that controls the temperature of the water, reducing the pressure of the hot or cold water if the other drops. It prevents scalding or freezing water from pouring out of the shower if someone else in the house operates another water-using appliance such as the kitchen sink or toilet.

Shower enclosures A shower cubicle must be well fitted and water resistant, and it is essential that you spend time and money ensuring that it remains so, as leaks can be an absolute devil to locate once they start. Water penetrating the surrounding surfaces will raise and spoil the rest of the surface and leak onto the area around and below the shower. Tiling is the only real option, even though it is expensive and time-consuming to effect. It's really worth the investment as simply painting the enclosure with an oil-based paint will only last a maximum of a year before contraction and expansion causes paint to crack and the shower to leak.

A beautiful and simply detailed wet room does away with the messiness of shower trays and cubicles.

Shower screens Shower screens come in a variety of styles, but on the whole, the simpler undecorated ones will fit into any bathroom more readily. Shower screens come in either sliding or hinged options. The former are good for small bathrooms where space is at a minimum, but the cheaper lower quality varieties can catch and jolt annoyingly. Hinged doors are the alternative, but make sure that the hinges prevent water from escaping. For a bath shower, you can purchase special hinged and sliding screens that fit to the side wall and top edge of your bath. This will be an efficient method of stopping water everywhere, but are more expensive than a simple rail and shower curtain system that drops into the bath.

You will find that, over time, your glass shower screen will become cloudy and dirty due to residues in the water – use a strong cleaning agent or limescale remover to keep it looking clean and clear.

A fabric shower screen is also another option and there are plenty of funky designs to choose from. Their main disadvantage is that they tend to get sucked into the shower by the updraught of warm air created by the hot water, making them stick unappealingly to your legs and body. Visually, a curtain never gives the same clean lines as a simple glass screen, but they are a far cheaper option if you are on a tight budget.

Wet rooms These are fully waterproofed bathrooms without enclosures that allow steam to fill the space and water to gush across the floor, giving a steam room feel to your shower. Although this may seem like an exciting and luxurious idea, you must remember two things. Firstly, your toilet paper will always be soggy and the floor difficult to keep clean due to the surface layer of water, and, secondly and more importantly, you must carefully consider the drainage details. For the wet room to work, water must flow down towards a drain, often located in the middle of the room. This will require building up the sides of the room above the level of the drain and is really best attempted when you can either dig the drainage system into the floor or raise the floor to allow for proper drainage. Wet rooms are invariably very costly to install because of the drainage details and the expanse of floor-to-ceiling tiles required, so are best tackled by those with a larger budget.

Additional features

If you have the space, make your bathroom a place to hang out. Additional furniture, such as a chair or floor cushions, can turn it into a place to spend peaceful time with your partner or by yourself. Make sure the room is well ventilated so that humidity won't build up and they won't suffer from damp.

In addition, putting plants in your bathroom increases the tactile and natural feel of the room, increasing its invigorating quality. Supplement this with various elements to heighten the sensory experience of your room – for example, aromatherapy oils and burners, candles, incense, bath oils, music or speakers linked to a stereo system in another room. All these will add to a more exciting, pleasurable and relaxing space.

Kitchens

An increasing interest in entertaining at home and our changing lifestyles mean that now, more than ever, kitchens are one of the key features of any house. Not only does the kitchen contribute greatly to the value of a property but it also tends to become the focal hub of a home. It therefore seems only appropriate that the kitchen demands a high level of thought and preparation in its design – particularly if you intend to keep within budget. And because there is only so long that you can eat take-out food for, it is one of the rooms that you will want to get finished fairly early on!

Planning With such a high level of importance of both function and potential cost, careful planning is essential before you go out and spend any of your hard-earned cash on a beautiful new kitchen. The functional aspects of your kitchen include storage, food preparation, cooking and basic hygiene, while the style aspects include worktops, flooring and cupboard fronts. It's in the planning that these two aspects will come together to create a space that you feel happy and relaxed working in. Food cooked in a good frame of mind is food that is a pleasure to eat.

With so many decisions to make, designing your kitchen can seem like an overwhelming task. It needn't be too complicated, however, if you take it step by step, follow a few basic but essential rules and understand the materials available to you and your budget.

The work triangle All the different activities that take place in the kitchen mean the layout of the various parts is crucial. It must be practical and well thought out to make it as efficient and easy to use as possible. Consider that in the basic preparation of food the necessary activities generally take place between three elements in the kitchen – the fridge, the sink and the cooker. It is essential that access between these three is kept clear and that there is workspace between each on which to progress the food preparation. All the other elements in the kitchen then need to be

TIP: Kitchens can be expensive rooms to completely redesign. For a quick but effective make-over, you may want to consider leaving the unit carcasses and appliances alone and simply think about replacing the splashbacks, worktops, unit fronts and flooring, or possibly just repaint the walls and install new lighting. Any of these ideas are effective low-budget ways of making a dramatic change to a kitchen.

laid out around these three basics. The relationship between them is known as the 'work triangle' and relates to the layout of every kitchen, whatever its shape (see diagrams opposite).

Think about the process of cooking a meal and you will start to understand the importance of the work triangle. First of all, you take the necessary ingredients from the fridge and place them on a surface nearby. Next, you would probably wash any fresh produce, so being near the sink and water is an advantage. You would probably then pile up the washed produce and other ingredients and store them temporarily near the hob or oven ready for chopping before cooking. In addition, you may need to drain food from boiling water so clear, unobstructed access to the sink will be necessary. Obviously this scenario does not match the preparation of all food but a clear layout with unobstructed movement and light will always make the kitchen a safer and easier place to cook.

The initial starting point when planning the kitchen generally lies in locating the soil (or waste) pipe for the sink. Once you have positioned the sink as close to this as necessary – you may need to talk to a plumber or builder about the fall or drop of this pipe – you can then begin to position the other elements to create the ideal work triangle arrangement.

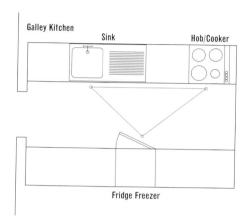

Galley Kitchen

Sink   Hob/Cooker

Fridge Freezer

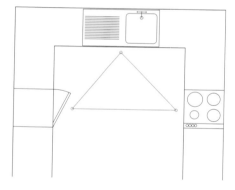

U Shaped Kitchen

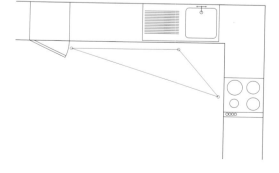

L Shaped Kitchen

Kitchen necessities

Storage and access are obviously major issues when designing your kitchen. There are many items you may need in the room and you should think carefully about what should go where for ease of use and safety:

▶ **Food** – dried foods, fresh fruit and vegetables, cans and packages, herbs and spices, refrigerated foods, frozen foods, drinks, alcohol

▶ **Appliances** – cooker, hob, sink/drainer, fridge, freezer, dishwasher, washing machine (and tumble drier), microwave oven

▶ **Utility items** – garbage bin, dustbin bags, cleaning products, kitchen roll/food wrap/foil, recycling area, lightbulbs, candles and matches, broom, mop and bucket, vacuum cleaner and vacuum bags, iron and ironing board, tea towels

▶ **Utensils/crockery** – everyday crockery, dinner service, cutlery, serving dishes, glassware, jugs and vases, decanters, pots and pans, cooking utensils, saucepans, cookware

▶ **Electrical equipment** – kettle, toaster, food processor, blender, juicer, fondue set

Costs and kitchen design There are various ways to acquire your kitchen, depending on your budget, the time you have to devote to the project, the way you want it to look and your do-it-yourself abilities:

▶ The most expensive and luxurious way to design a kitchen is to talk to a specialist kitchen designer who, with the assistance of computer-aided design programmes, can help you fully visualize the final design as well as suggest a variety of possibilities. Although costly, this is probably the most efficient way as the designer can help you to utilize every spare inch of space and advise on ideal arrangements and space-saving fittings.

▶ A slightly cheaper option would be to use a do-it-yourself store that offers a more limited design service, and can then sell you flat-packed kitchen units and organize kitchen fitters. Again, the retailer should be able to sell you space-saving units and carousels to make use of even the most difficult-to-reach corners.

▶ The cheapest option is for you to plan and design your own kitchen, and buy flat-packed units for assembly by you or a local carpenter or builder. It is not too difficult but you will need to think carefully about the dimensions, your needs and your budget.

▶ Alternatively, you could buy freestanding units. These offer greater flexibility in the layout of your kitchen, but give a more temporary look to the room. However, the added advantage is that you can always take the units with you when you move house.

If you are considering planning and ordering a kitchen by yourself, you must measure the room carefully and decide on the kitchen units before you make your purchase. The reason for this is that kitchen units come in a relatively limited selection of sizes so you will have to arrange the various widths of cupboards, drawers and shelves carefully in order to fill the space to maximum efficiency. Any odd leftover spaces can be filled by blank panels, but good planning will help you to minimize this wasted space.

You need to draw a plan indicating not only the widths of the units and the distances the unit doors may open but also elevations of the walls in order to show the locations and heights of units. Remember to include on your plan:

▶ Doors and windows – their heights and the direction they swing open

▶ Radiator heights and widths

▶ The location of the waste water outlet (near an external wall for drainage)

▶ Water inlet pipes

▶ The location of the gas inlet pipe

▶ The location of existing electrical sockets – ordinary ones and spurs (fixed electrical sockets for items like the cooker)

▶ Any other features such as the electric fuse box, gas, electric or water meters

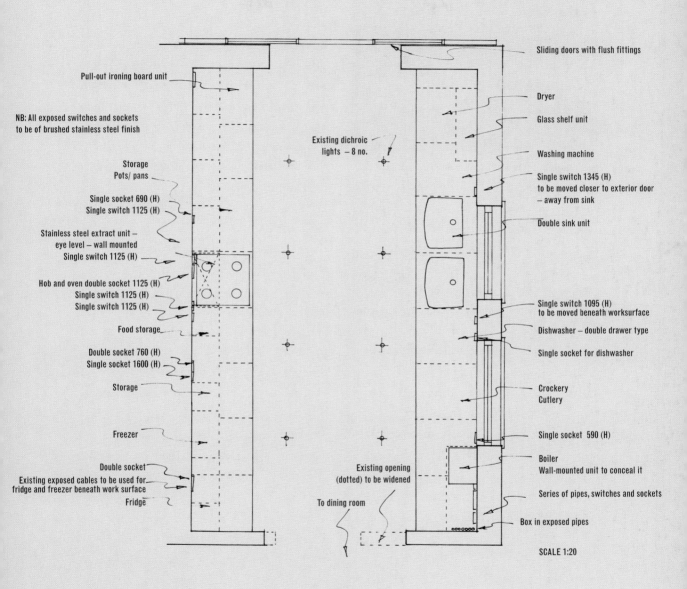

Pull-out ironing board unit

NB: All exposed switches and sockets to be of brushed stainless steel finish

Storage
Pots/ pans

Single socket 690 (H)
Single switch 1125 (H)

Stainless steel extract unit –
eye level – wall mounted
Single switch 1125 (H)

Hob and oven double socket 1125 (H)
Single switch 1125 (H)
Single switch 1125 (H)

Food storage

Double socket 760 (H)
Single socket 1600 (H)

Storage

Freezer

Double socket
Existing exposed cables to be used for
fridge and freezer beneath work surface
Fridge

Existing dichroic
lights – 8 no.

Existing opening
(dotted) to be widened

To dining room

Sliding doors with flush fittings

Dryer

Glass shelf unit

Washing machine

Single switch 1345 (H)
to be moved closer to exterior door
– away from sink

Double sink unit

Single switch 1095 (H)
to be moved beneath worksurface

Dishwasher – double drawer type

Single socket for dishwasher

Crockery
Cutlery

Single socket 590 (H)

Boiler
Wall-mounted unit to conceal it

Series of pipes, switches and sockets

Box in exposed pipes

SCALE 1:20

Plan out your kitchen carefully, drawing it to scale.

Remember the electrical, plumbing, lighting, storage, cooking

and practical needs that have to be incorporated.

Make use of every space by using clever specially designed units where possible.

Layout of your units Unless you have a purpose-built larder, units will probably provide the bulk of the storage space in your kitchen, and crockery, cutlery, food, cooking utensils and appliances will all have to be accommodated within them. With all the appliances you may need in your kitchen and the needs of your work triangle, you may be left with very little additional space for storage so you must make use of every available area.

Start by considering the layout of your base units and how you will integrate your work triangle of fridge, sink and cooker, allowing some worksurface preparation area between each. Next, consider the most convenient location for your pots, pans and cooking utensils – probably next to the cooker. Position the crockery and cutlery storage areas somewhere near the sink and dishwasher, if you have one, to make putting all the items away after washing-up much less of a chore. Make the most of inconvenient corners by using sliding units or rotating carousels.

Generally, base units come in a standard dimension of 60 cm deep x 60 cm wide (24 x 24 in), which accommodate most standard kitchen appliances within them. Wall-mounted eye-level units, however, tend to be only 35 cm (14 in) deep, so are appropriate for storing food, cups, glasses and some crockery, but not pots and pans or sharp utensils. They should, as a rule, be at least 40 cm (16 in) above the worksurface and allow for task lighting, which can cast a good clear light over the surface.

An alternative to eye-level units with doors is to have open shelves. This creates a more relaxed look, which can be used to display crockery but will need to be cleaned regularly to prevent the build-up of dirt and grease.

Remember that ventilation is essential in a kitchen and the inclusion of an extraction fan above the hob is a legal requirement in many countries. This prevents the build-up of smells and sticky cooking residues. It generally consists of the extraction unit, which needs electrical power, and a hood – normally made of glass or metal – to catch the gases. There are two types of extraction unit – one that cleans the air in a filter and returns it to the kitchen, and another that pushes the air outside via a flue. The latter is more efficient, but inevitably more costly to purchase and fit as you will need a builder to cut and fit the pipe from the unit through the exterior wall to vent the air outside away from a window that opens.

Lighting

In such a high-activity area as the kitchen, lighting plays a key part in the safety and function of the room, helping you prepare food in a safe working environment and ensure that it's properly cooked. To do this, you need to consider lighting the main areas of activity as well as the general area of the kitchen.

General lighting You need good clean lighting over the entire kitchen floor area, leaving no dark patches. This might best be achieved with a series of ceiling-mounted spotlights spread across the ceiling. Alternatively, you could have a number of pendant lights hanging down to provide good even lighting. Whatever your final choice, the general point to remember is that you will need more than one centrally mounted light to light the room properly and safely. Single lights tend to cast shadows across the room, which can be dangerous. For a more flexible lighting scheme, fit your lights with dimmer switches to help create mood and atmosphere when you aren't preparing food.

Task lighting This plays an important part in your kitchen as it lights the more dangerous and tricky tasks of chopping and preparing food. Good task lighting throws clear unobstructed light directly onto your hands. This is most easily achieved by fixing lights to the underside of your eye-level units and

concealing the cables carefully. Most units have integrated lighting to help with cooking, but you will need additional lights for the rest of the worksurfaces. All kitchen retailers sell under-mounted lights – halogen spotlights, slim-line fluorescent strip lights or tungsten bulb fittings. Whatever the style, make sure they are encased and have the correct safety rating to avoid the risk of electric shock.

If under-mounted lights are not possible, you could have ceiling-mounted pendant lights hanging directly above the worksurfaces or even clip-on lights fixed at a high level to shine down, although these will collect dirt and grease more readily than encased lights.

Think carefully about where you will need different types of lighting such as onto worksurfaces and the floor.

Flooring

Due to its high level of use and the frequency with which it will need to be washed, flooring in a kitchen has to be considered carefully. If you are installing a kitchen in an area with another function such as a dining space you may also wish to zone the kitchen work area by changing the flooring and use it as an opportunity to lay down a more hardwearing surface. (See 'Flooring', pages 70–85, for more detail on the different types of flooring available.)

Solid wood Because wood is a natural material it is susceptible to changes in air moisture content. It therefore needs regular attention and must be sealed carefully from the outset when used in a kitchen to protect it from spillages, stains and normal wear and tear. It is, of course, possible to use solid wood in a kitchen but you should bear in mind that if you had a flood in the room it might cause the floor to twist and warp.

Engineered laminate flooring This is a cheaper alternative to solid wood with the added advantage that the flooring often comes prefinished, saving you the hard work of sealing it. Check with the supplier before you buy to make sure that the flooring is suitable for use in a kitchen as the presence of excess water – for example, a burst pipe or a washing machine flood – can make some engineered laminates come apart.

MDF-backed laminate flooring It is strongly advised not to use this now prolific and cheap flooring in kitchens as the MDF (medium-density fibreboard) backing reacts badly to water, swelling and separating from the plastic top layer. It has the potential to ruin at the first drop of excess water or spillage.

Stone Available from flooring specialists in a vast range of styles, this is a beautiful, hardwearing but costly solution to kitchen flooring. Be sure to use coloured grout to hide stains and marks. The main disadvantage is that it is a very unforgiving surface and any delicate object that is dropped on it will smash.

Tiles Again, there is a vast selection of tiles available, many of which mimic natural stone to very convincing effect. Glazed tiles do not require sealing but unglazed ones will need to be sealed or oiled to prevent stains and marks.

A solid wooden floor will wear beautifully and give a relaxed, organic feel to your kitchen.

Rubber This effective and fun finish for a kitchen is hardwearing, easy to clean and totally waterproof. The vast range of colours available means it is easy to match rubber flooring with the other elements that make up your kitchen. Note that heavily textured rubber flooring tends to trap the dirt, so pick a smooth or low-relief textured finish. For a more professional look you could investigate the option of a poured rubber floor. The advantage here is that it has no joins so will give a seamless waterproof finish.

Metal For the industrial look, go for checker-plate aluminium flooring. This can be bought in either sheet form or, more conveniently, tile form. It is hardwearing but expensive, cold to the touch and not easy to fit, particularly if you have an irregularly shaped kitchen. Again, any delicate objects will smash if they land on this flooring.

Linoleum Again, this comes in a variety of colours and styles and offers a relatively cheap solution for kitchen flooring. In addition, it is warm underfoot, very resistant to marks and stains and requires very little maintenance.

Vinyl Probably the cheapest kitchen flooring available, vinyl comes in a massive range of colours and styles, as well as simulating other types of materials such as wood and stone. Make sure you purchase a high-quality vinyl that is made from pure PVC as cheaper varieties are more brittle and susceptible to staining over longer periods of time.

Cork A great solution for cheap, effective and natural kitchen flooring. Cork is easy to cut and fit and can be stained to give a more contemporary look. It is also waterproof and, providing you seal it properly, will be stain resistant.

Furniture and Fittings

An essential part of the look and practicality of your kitchen will come from the basic furniture and fittings, such as work tops, cupboard fronts and handles, splash backs, sinks and taps. These are elements that will need to be thought about to coordinate the overall style and that you will need to interact with on a daily basis. So think about how easy they will be to use when you are busy in your kitchen, and how proud you will feel when you stand back and show off your kitchen to your friends!

Worktops These are going to be one of the most important visual aspects of your kitchen, as well as one of the most tactile elements. In general, the advice is to spend money on your worksurfaces as they will raise the whole standard of the kitchen. There is a wide variety on the market to suit a range of budgets so it is worth looking carefully at just how much you can afford.

Stone is one of the most stylish options for a kitchen surface, but also one of the most costly. There are several types of stone that you can choose from, and each has benefits and handicaps. **Granite** is one of the toughest, has a cool, sleek feeling and is incredibly durable. Polished surfaces can look ostentatious so my advice would be to go for a matt (or honed) surface. **Marble** is cool to touch, individual-looking and great for making pastry on, but it is porous so will stain easily. As it is relatively soft, it scratches and marks easily so is not generally recommended but you could be careful with it and use a chopping board rather than cut directly onto it. **Slate** is a dark grey stone similar in appearance to granite but much softer and more porous so it will stain and scratch. A matt or honed finish is more durable, provided you use a chopping board. **Limestone** is another popular but soft and porous material. Its light colour means it is easily stained and you need to be careful when using abrasive cleaners. At least once a year you will need to use a powerful cleaner on it to remove scuffs and stains, then apply a stain stop. This is a colourless liquid that won't affect the colour, but will prevent excessive marking. This high level of maintenance, and its porosity, means that limestone is not often recommended by manufacturers.

Plastic composites (e.g. Corian) are extremely versatile, man-made materials that are non-porous and won't stain. They are long-lasting and hardwearing, and any scratches can be sanded out. They come in many finishes but often the simplest plain colours are the best. One of their great advantages is that they can be seamlessly welded together so you end up with a smooth surface with no unsightly joins. They are, however, still very expensive.

Concrete is now one of the most exciting materials for producing one-off bespoke kitchen worksurfaces. It generally has to be cast in situ so is messy but gives you the opportunity to cast objects such as sinks and hobs into the surface. It is extremely heavy so check that your floors and units will be able to take the weight. Once the concrete is cast, it must be left to cure for approximately two weeks before it can be sealed with a resin based sealant. This will be carried out by your specialist concrete contractor, but will only need to be applied once.

Stainless steel is the ultimate for the professional industrial look and is hardwearing and easy to maintain. It can discolour but bleaching regularly will help. Stainless steel will scratch but this can lead to an impressive patina that suggests you really are a professional chef! One advantage is that it runs seamlessly into elements such as sinks and drainers. Make sure that you take your dimensions carefully or get the manufacturer to measure up as it is difficult to alter once made. Prices vary massively, but are becoming more affordable as retailers realize the popularity.

Solid wood has a natural feel that gives kitchens a beautifully wholesome feeling. Wooden worktops are hardwearing but need care and attention as water can penetrate the finish and discolour the wood. It is advisable to apply waxes and oils to the surfaces regularly. Scratches can also be sanded back thus making it a long-lasting surface. Try to go for hardwoods as softwoods require a lot more maintenance. Prices vary, so shop around and look for as thick a worksurface as possible for a greater visual weight and quality. When choosing your worktop, make sure that the wood, whether hard or soft, is from an FSC (Forest Stewardship Council)-recognized sustainable source (see 'Reuse', page 241).

Laminate (e.g. Formica) is one of the cheapest options. Available in a huge variety of colours and styles, it is always going to be popular for kitchens. Laminate is basically a sheet of tough plastic glued to a backing board, generally chipboard or MDF (medium-density fibreboard). Make sure you choose a high-pressure laminate for a hardwearing, long-lasting and heat-resistant worktop. Low-pressure laminates have a thinner plastic and should only be used in low-wear situations such as the insides of cupboards. A great, flexible, funky option for worktops, you can even get layered laminates that have a top surface of brushed steel to give a version of the stainless steel worktop.

Ceramic tiles are a relatively cheap and easy way to add a unique touch to your kitchen. With such a vast range of colours and styles, you can really imprint your own identity. You could even think about using broken fragments for a mosaic finish. However, tiled surfaces are very difficult to keep clean, hygienically and visually, and the grout tends to attract dirt and fragments of food that are difficult to wipe free. If you are going to use tiles in the kitchen, make sure that you use a grey or coloured grout, which shows dirt and marks less readily.

Cupboard doors and drawer fronts These are going to determine the overall look for your kitchen. Remember that you will be choosing fronts for both the base and the eye-level units, so you may want them all to match, to vary slightly or even to contrast – for example, laminates on the base units and glass-fronted eye-level units.

There is a huge variety of different unit-front styles on the market so choosing the right one can be hard. Bear in mind that smooth flat fronts rather than panelled ones trap less dirt and are easier to clean, plus they have a more contemporary feel. Also, fronts with a high-gloss finish or glass doors reflect available light from a window into darker areas of your kitchen. Ultimately, it is up to personal taste and will say something about you, whether you go for contemporary, traditional, country cottage-style, glass or laminates:

▶ **Solid wood** – there are a variety of styles and types available that offer a choice of colour and wood grain effect. They generally come with durable ready-finished lacquered surfaces, but remember that have highly decorative surfaces will be harder to clean.

▶ **Veneers** – a thin slice of wood is glued to a MDF (medium-density fibreboard) or chipboard backing, which is then varnished or lacquered. Cheaper because of their lower wood content, veneers offer a more exciting range of woods and with a better grain.

Think about the combinations of materials that make up your kitchen, mix them carefully for a unique personalised look.

with a hard-wearing and wipeable paint, such as an oil based eggshell or a specialist kitchen paint. This is a relatively short term solution, however, as the cabinet fronts will need to be repainted or touched up each year.

▶ **Laminates** – these come in a variety of colours and styles.

▶ **Lacquers** – these are very high quality, expensive finishes that consist of multiple hard wearing layers of high gloss paint with a mirror like finish. They are sprayed onto an MDF base and come in many colours.

▶ **Metallic** – there are a variety of styles and types – from aluminium to zinc and stainless steel. Metallic fronts generally comprise a thin layer of metal stuck onto a wooden surface.

▶ **Glass** – this can be textured, etched or ribbed and is an exciting contemporary material for kitchens, but make sure it is toughened for strength.

▶ **Paint** – the cheapest option if you are on a budget, allowing you to revamp old units easily. Make sure you prepare the surfaces properly by sanding and priming them. If you are painting onto plastic laminate, use a melamine primer as an undercoat before you add paint. This should then be overpainted

Handles Door and drawer handles can add a great decorative element to your kitchen. There is a huge range of prices and varieties on the market and they can be a great way to personalize and improve the look of your kitchen if you go for cheaper doors and units. Always choose handles that are easy to operate – particularly for when you are midway through cooking. Flour, fish and egg yolk, for example, are unpleasant elements to be left on difficult-to-clean handles!

The options for handles include:

▶ **Long horizontal handles** – horizontal styles such as steel bars improve the horizontal lines of the kitchen, making it appear longer.

▶ **Recessed handles** – these are cut into doors and drawers and give a minimal designer feel.

▶ **Surface-mounted pulls or knobs** – these can look cluttered and are slightly more difficult to use being smaller and more fiddly.

A good idea for eye-level units is to extend the door below the bottom of the cabinet, making it easy to grab the door and pull it open without a handle. Whatever you decide on, do have a look at the handles in a well-stocked supplier or do-it-yourself store, as choosing them from a catalogue can be deceptive as they may feel a lot cheaper in real life.

Alternatively, if you want to be really unique, you could think about making your own amusing or stylish handles. Consider bent metal forks, beaded string, lengths of rope, straps made from leather or suede offcuts, even hooks that double as handles.

Taps and sinks Taps come in a wide variety of styles and finishes to suite every budget and taste. It is generally best to fit a mixer tap instead of a set of taps for ease of use. This comes with either two separate taps or a single lever arm that is used to turn the taps on and adjust the temperature. For ease of cleaning you could go for a wall-mounted spout and taps, to free up your work surface and prevent dirt from getting trapped, but this will be more costly to fit and service.

Your choice of sink will again reflect the style of kitchen you have opted for and there are several options to choose from:

These antique style mixer taps work well in this pared-down, functional style kitchen.

▶ **Plastic** – these come in a wide variety of shapes and colours. Plastic sinks are inexpensive and scratch resistant but do discolour and look cheap after a little while.

▶ **Synthetic** – these sinks are made from a variety of materials such as resin, plastic and stone particles, and are therefore often known as composite sinks. They are hardwearing and durable, and come in a variety of colours.

▶ **Stainless steel** – available in many shapes, stainless steel sinks are easy to maintain and durable. The thicker the gauge of the steel, the less noise the sink will make and the less it will bend – 18 gauge is sufficient for domestic use, thinner gauge such as 20 or 22 is noisier.

▶ **Ceramic** – the traditional style of kitchen sink (such as the Belfast sink), these are now being produced in contemporary styles and can look great in new or old-style kitchens. They have a great sense of quality and style, but can be very expensive. They are also unforgiving if you happen to drop a glass into them!

Whatever your budget and choice of sink, for a sleeker feel, go for one that is fixed to the underside of the worksurface, as opposed to a surface-mounted sink, which will trap water and dirt around the surface lip. Whether you opt for a single or double sink is a matter of personal preference. If you have the space, a double sink can be useful in order to make washing vegetables or doing the washing up easier.

In addition, you need to consider the style of drainer as you will inevitably need somewhere to place items you have washed up to allow the water to drain off into the sink. If you have chosen a stone or moulded worksurface, you can have the drainer worked into the surface. If not, buy either a separate freestanding drainer or a sink with an integrated drainer for ease of use.

An under-mounted sink and surface-mounted taps will give a neat, efficient and sleek look to your work surface.

Splashbacks These are an essential feature required to catch any liquid that splashes from the sink, cooker or worktops. A splashback can be as simple as a painted surface – in eggshell or gloss paint for a wipeable finish – but you may want to consider a surface that is tougher and more resistant to heat, water, knocks and scrapes. Being a vertical surface it constitutes a major aspect to the look of your kitchen and, as such, must be easy to clean and maintain.

▶ **Stainless steel** – this will provide a highly professional look, is costly to purchase and fit, but durable and easy to maintain. For a cheaper metal option, purchase a sheet of steel cut to the right dimensions, clean it thoroughly with wire wool and coat in a clear lacquer to protect it from rusting, then glue or screw it to your wall.

▶ **Stone** – again, this is costly to purchase and fit but, coordinated with a stone worksurface, will give the kitchen a quality finish. For a cheaper option, take the stone only 12–15 cm (5–6 in) up the wall as this is the area that gets the most wear. Paint the rest of the splashback area above that.

▶ **Glass** – for a slick designer look, get an enamelled glass splashback. With this material the glass is back painted and then heated to toughen the paint. This is relatively cost-efficient and can be ordered in a range of colours. Its reflective surface will bounce any available light around the room.

▶ **Laminates** – these are a possibility but ensure that they are kept away from excessive heat such as is found near to the cooker as they can melt.

▶ **Tiles** or **mosaics** – you can create a unique look for your kitchen through your choice of tiles or mosaic pieces. Be sure to use a coloured grout between the tiles as white will inevitably show up dirt and stains from food splashes.

Bins and recycling With such a long list of elements that need to be incorporated into the kitchen it's easy for the humble garbage bin to be forgotten. However, what we throw out has now become a more relevant issue and with doorstep collection of recycled materials becoming increasingly common it is now easier than ever before to separate out and dispose of your rubbish properly. This is particularly relevant in the kitchen as you use more packaging here than in any other room in the house, but it does mean that we need to accommodate larger storage for our waste.

Many kitchen retailers now sell multi-sectioned bins that fit into kitchen units or in pull-out drawers. This allows you to separate cans, glass, paper and plastics into sections as you throw them away. As these sections are inevitably smaller than a conventional bin, it's also a good idea to find some other space in your home – for example, under the stairs – to store recycling items ready for collection or for you to take to the recycling depot (see also 'Recycle', pages 242–3).

Other bin options for the kitchen include:
▶ Plastic or metal swing bins
▶ Flip-top metal cylinder bins
▶ Under-the-sink, swing-out bins
▶ Compost bins – for organic waste to use as compost in the garden
▶ Galvanized small-scale dustbins

As one of the more public rooms in your home, your lounge is a multi-functional area that says a lot about you and your style, and also incorporates activities such as relaxation, entertainment and entertaining. However, this range of activity means that your lounge will require a high level of flexibility to allow all these activities to occur within the one space.

As this is a room whose function often centres around social activities, the idea of a visual focus is as important as ever. Because we are now less likely to have the benefit of a real fire as the centrepiece for our lounge, we have to think a bit harder about how we can create a central feature around which furniture can be arranged.

Your lounge should be somewhere that you are proud to take people, that says something about who you are, and has the flexibility to cater for every situation – from a night in with your friends to a visit from the in-laws.

A multi-functional room

Consider all the different functions of your lounge. Writing a list often helps you realize the range of activities that it has to cater for:

► Socializing with friends and family
► Relaxing after a hard day
► Reading or listening to music
► Eating
► Romantic interludes
► Watching television
► Hangover recovery
► Lazy Sundays
► Playing with the kids/having somewhere separate for the kids to play!
► Displaying your favourite objects/photos/collections
► Playing games/computer games
► Spare/guest bedroom

Planning Drawing a plan (see 'Understanding your space', pages 13–16) will help you decide on the furniture you want and the materials you'll have to purchase. If you draw the furniture on paper and cut each piece out, you can rearrange them easily without having to shift them around. Remember that the room needs a visual focus, a clear circulation path, a sense of social interaction and warmth, and that natural light mustn't affect activities such as watching television.

Furniture and lighting are two key areas where you can incorporate flexibility to allow for the various functions of the lounge.

Your furniture arrangements should allow for different activities to occur. For instance, a lounge that has a sofa, two armchairs, floor cushions and a thick rug offers a variety of seating options. It allows for formal socializing and relaxed lounging around. In addition, movable pieces of furniture such as floor cushions and swivelling armchairs can allow you to easily reorientate the focus of your room – for example, from watching television to socializing.

Flexibility in the lighting in the room should allow for concentrated activities such as reading and writing to occur efficiently, and also allow for times of relaxation, especially by using dimmer switches on overhead lights and table lamps and candles to create a softer, gentler atmosphere.

Create a warm sociable focus to your lounge using furniture, fabrics, rugs and colour and lighting.

Use your walls and dressings to create a textural identity to your lounge that will offer warmth and focus.

On a more practical level, you need to consider what audio-visual equipment has to go where and make sure you have sufficient electric sockets to allow this to happen safely. You will probably want to incorporate a television, video and DVD players, and maybe a computer games and stereo system. You will also need additional electric sockets in other areas of the room to allow for side lights and feature lights that will give the room a greater sense of balance and atmosphere.

Layout and focus The layout of your lounge will depend largely on the existing architectural form and features of the space. These include the door, fireplace, windows and orientation. It's up to you to decide what you want as the visual focus for your lounge – texture, light, objects or entertainment. Having a strong focus will give the area character and identity and create a visual anchoring point around which other elements in the room can then be organized.

Historically, a fireplace with its flickering flames and golden embers would have created the focus; nowadays there is a tendency for the television to be the centrepiece of a room. Although this might provide a large amount of your entertainment, do you really want your television to be the visual focus of the room at all times? While being viewed, the television reduces social interaction to a lower level and when it's turned off, it is simply a black box that offers nothing in terms of focus. The television is inevitably an important element in many people's lives and it's important to find a way to incorporate it into the room but remember that a more substantial visual focus will be needed to anchor your design. You could think about buying or making a cabinet for the television or simply draping material over it when it is not being used.

A visual focus or centrepiece is more generally a wall-based piece, or even a series of objects, that takes the place of the traditional fireplace. Your visual focus could be:

▶ A dramatic feature light, such as a lava lamp or ball of twinkling fairy lights

▶ A stunning piece of artwork

▶ A treasured object – natural materials, a bought item or even something you've made

▶ A variety of objects that have similarities yet subtle differences, such as a collection of glass vases or mosaic artwork

In addition to your visual focus, you may incorporate within the lounge elements for display that portray influences of personal taste, identity or history. These could be treasured items, heirlooms, bought pieces, artworks, collections or natural objects of beauty, which could be displayed on surfaces such as shelves, sideboards, side tables, plinths or windowsills. Probably more than many other rooms in the house, your lounge will be a public space that will provide the main opportunity for you to display your sense of identity through your domestic design style.

On a final note, and on a greater scale, it is important to think about acoustic privacy both inside and outside your lounge. There are a number of elements in the lounge that produce noise – for example, the television and stereo, as well as activities such as reading and watching television that could be disturbed by noise in another room. If you are considering knocking down walls so as to have a single open-plan kitchen-diner-living space, do think about noise spillage (or noise pollution) as a variety of people in the household carrying out different activities in an open-plan space may well produce conflict. Having a separate lounge will allow different activities within the home to occur at the same time. Think very carefully about which activities you really want going on in the same room before you set to work with your sledgehammer!

Lighting

Lighting As your lounge that has a variety of uses at different times of the day, the lighting will need a lot of flexibility to allow you to alter the atmosphere, mood and function. This can be created easily and cheaply by a good lighting system that allows you to go from bright and functional to warm and cosy at the flick of a switch or two. Creating a flexible lighting system will allow you to enjoy everything that you want your lounge to be.

Natural light This can be the most wonderful source of energy and colour for your lounge. Although natural light is always a benefit in any room, in this case it can be a hindrance for the location of your television, which will pick up reflections and glare from light streaming in. You will probably need to think about some type of screening to control this and to offer an element of privacy from the street in what is very often the front room of the house. Views into the room should also be restricted for means of security – a variety of audio-visual equipment on show can be a great incentive for the casual thief looking for a quick job. You may want to screen only the bottom half of the window, which you can do with self-adhesive frosted-glass effect film, sheer curtains or sill-mounted blinds that pull up (see 'Window dressings', pages 94–9).

General lighting It's important to have good general lighting for the whole room. Traditionally this would have been achieved with a centrally mounted pendant hanging from the ceiling. The main problem with this is that most of the activities in the room happen around the perimeter and so generally occur in the shadow of the main light. If this is your only option, make sure you supplement the lighting with additional lights such as task lights. Alternatively, you could get an electrician to attach several longer cables to the light and suspend them from hooks in the corners of the room to reflect light off the walls.

You could consider using wall- or floor-mounted uplighters to bounce a softer light off the ceiling, or you could use an even spread of halogen or tungsten lights across the ceiling to cast an even light across the whole floor.

A variety of lighting types will give your lounge warmth, character and flexibility.

Task lighting Side tables or other surfaces present an opportunity to position task lights in areas of activity, such as at one end of a sofa or next to an armchair where you may want to read. Task lights may also be freestanding standard lamps that can throw light over the shoulder of a chair, giving a pool of light and a sense of elegance to the room. Task lights of one sort or another, be they spotlights or table lamps, can provide gentle pools of light, which are controlled by the lampshades you use. Lighter coloured shades tend to throw cooler light around the room while darker ones control the light more and produce a warm glow around them. In effect, your task lights will start to act as decorative lights and can greatly affect the atmosphere of the room.

Decorative lighting This is a must to give mood, atmosphere and a sense of fun (and romance) to your lounge. Lights from the humble candle to more elaborate fibreoptic systems can provide the visual focus once offered by a real fire, and you could also consider using light boxes, rope lights, fairy lights and side lamps with low-wattage bulbs to create something really special.

Walls Together with window dressings, furniture, cushions, flooring and lighting, walls are part of the layered effect that will become the look of your lounge. There are really no restrictions as to what you can choose.

You can use a wall treatment to create a visual focus in the room – for example, by using wallpaper or stencilling to create a feature wall around which you can arrange the furniture. This can, in turn, provide the basis for the colour scheme in the room if you pick out a base colour or accent from within the wallpaper's design. You can use this to create a relaxing tonal scheme for your lounge but you may, on the other hand, wish to inject a little energy into the space by choosing an accent or a contrasting colour scheme, which can lead to dynamic and exciting results.

Remember to consider the layering effect of your walls and how else you may use them by devoting a certain amount of wall area to

Even the simplest artistic wall panels will add visual interest and texture to your lounge.

displaying pictures, photos and objects on shelves. These may be individual items or arranged in groups or clusters.

Your choice of colours may also be determined by an existing piece of furniture such as a sofa or an armchair but if you can change this, it's best to think of the colour you want to live with and then attempt either to re-cover the offending piece of furniture or to use a throw to recolour it.

TIP: For a quick transformation, create a feature wall with a complementary wall colour or wallpaper and change the soft furnishings (such as cushion covers and curtains) to alter the look of your lounge without spending much money.

Flooring

Flooring You can use any one of a variety of flooring options in your lounge, depending on personal preference (see 'Flooring', pages 70–85, for more information), but, as always, bear in mind the style you are aiming for.

While carpet might be desirable and perceived as more luxurious, by contemporary standards it can feel stuffy, cluttered and outdated. A more exciting look may be to combine the relative ease of hardwood flooring with the focused softness of rugs. Your flooring options are likely to include the following:

▶ **Carpet** – the traditional option but it will collect dust, producing allergies and potentially clogging up electronic equipment.

▶ **Whip-stitched rugs** – standard carpets with the edges sewn up. Their advantage is that they come in many colours and piles, and are cheap when compared to purpose-made rugs.

▶ **Natural fibre carpeting** – pick from coir, jute or sea grass. These natural fibre carpets

Clever use of flooring materials will help to pull a room together suggesting a focus for activity and relaxation.

offer a contemporary organic solution to your lounge carpeting dilemma.

▶ **Solid flooring** – this hardwearing option may be the answer but can make the room seem cold and unwelcoming with a lack of visual focus to the seating area unless used in conjunction with a floor rug of some type.

▶ **Engineered floors** – a more affordable version of solid wood floors, while retaining many of the natural qualities of solid flooring.

▶ **Laminates** – a cheaper version of solid and engineered floors, these are both easy to lay and maintain.

TIPS:

Whip-stitched carpet offers you a massive variety of colours and textures, and is relatively cheap compared with buying a rug of a similar size. Your carpet retailer will be able to recommend whip-stitchers to finish off the edges of your carpet-rug.

An echo-like acoustic to a room will give the impression of a large, cold and uninviting space. If you are going to have hard surfaces on the floors and walls, remember to add some level of soft furnishings – rugs, cushions and curtains – to make the room sound warmer.

Storage It's only a lounge, but when you think about it, it's surprising just how many items need to be stored here. Many of these will be visually unsightly, and you will want to display some as decorative pieces, so having a combination of storage types may suit the style of your lounge as well as reducing clutter.

Consider the following list of items that you may well want to keep in the lounge but not necessarily see at all times:

► Television, video player, DVD player, satellite/cable box
► Stereo and speakers
► Computer games system
► CDs, cassettes, records, videotapes, DVDs
► Books, magazines and newspapers
► Games and toys

Although they have an important role in your lounge, many of these may not be the most beautiful things to look at and some need cabling, which can be messy. Think about storage that allows easy access on a daily basis and occasional access, as well as cable management systems, if necessary. These can be in the form of flexible plastic tubes that have been cut down one side to allow cables to be tucked inside, or simply plastic ties that hold a bundle of cables together.

While your television has to be at eye level in relation to your sofa, other electronic elements need to be positioned so that they can be operated by remote controls. Individual pieces of storage furniture offer the greatest level of efficiency for your room but you can also buy efficient purpose-built storage and display items such in the form of shelves and cupboards from most high-street shops.

TIP: Make sure that you have enough electrical sockets in the right place for all your technological needs. Do-it-yourself wiring or overloading sockets can be dangerous and having a spaghetti of cables strewn across the floor is hazardous and unsightly. If you don't have enough sockets, get an electrician in.

Furniture

Before you buy any furniture, check carefully that it will fit through the door and along corridors or stairs. Large pieces of furniture can be heavy and inflexible, and there is nothing that makes the confident designer look more stupid than having a three-seater sofa stuck in the doorway! It may seem obvious, but use your tape measure first.

Sofas With a sofa you have to think about the size of the space that it needs to fit into. You should leave enough room so that it doesn't feel squeezed in or squashed up against a wall and so that you can move around it. Scale is very important here. While it is tempting to just go for the biggest sofa you can afford, you must respect the dimensions of the area – it will make the room seem much more cluttered and cramped.

The way the sofa looks is obviously also important because you need to consider the overall look of the room. It's much better to opt for a simply styled sofa, which will offer greater flexibility if you wish to change your lounge later on or move home. A relatively neutral-coloured, plain sofa can be made to look different more readily by simply changing the cushions or throws that you put on it. These styling items can give the right level of visual detail to your sofa without making it overimpact on the space.

You also need to think about the wear and tear of the sofa. Light-coloured sofas show up dirt more readily while patterns hide the dirt but can clash with the rest of the room. For a hardwearing piece of furniture, choose a sofa with removable covers or a surface like leather, which can be wiped clean.

When designing your lounge, think about the arrangement of your furniture and the effect this will have on the way that people interact with one another. If you have a room large enough for two sofas, consider these basic arrangements:

▶ **Parallel** – positioning two sofas directly opposite each other can have a confrontational effect as people sit and face each other, which can seem uncomfortable.

▶ **L-shaped** – positioning one sofa at right angles to the other creates a more relaxed social situation and puts people at greater ease.

▶ **U-shaped arrangements** – this is another more relaxed and less confrontational arrangement that encourages conversation and relaxation, although it is only possible with more pieces of furniture.

Different types of seating offer your lounge a relaxed feeling and a sense of fun. In this room the variety of textures also help to give it an air of liveability and enjoyment.

Armchairs It can be a great pleasure to have a favourite armchair – a place you retire to at the end of the day or curl up in on a Sunday morning to read the paper. The right armchair can add depth and interest to your room – for example, an old leather armchair that has age and character. If you are looking for something newer, remember that an armchair can offer flexibility to your room if it is on wheels or swivels, allowing you to change the focus of the space. Having sofas and armchairs offers a less formal arrangement to the area than simply having two sofas.

Floor cushions, bean bags, pouffes and stools Generally seen as more contemporary forms of seating, these offer a chance to slouch and lounge around. They will make your room look more relaxed and less formal, but don't make the mistake of thinking this is the only furniture you need and buying them because they are relatively inexpensive. Regard them instead as items that add fun and flexibility to your space, but which also serve as a great supplement to other pieces of furniture.

Side/occasional tables Although these may seem an unnecessary expense, side tables are useful for breaking down the scale of larger pieces of furniture such as sofas. In addition, they become invaluable for styling objects and positioning side lamps, which are great for reading and mood-enhancing lighting. If you get tables of the right height in relation to your sofas and chairs, they can become useful occasional tables for a more relaxed form of dining.

Soft furnishings and styling items This is the final and most flexible layer of your lounge, without which your room won't be properly dressed. A well-styled lounge emanates a sense of warmth and invitation that will make the room hospitable and a pleasure to be in. Soft furnishings and styling items also provide an opportunity for you to express your ideas, interests, collections and identity as a designed layer across the space.

Soft furnishings such as rugs, throws, cushions and curtains also soak up the acoustics in a room so that it produces fewer echoes, giving the space a warmer, more intimate feel. There are also a number of styling objects that may help you to complete the look of your lounge (see box below). You may wish to go back to your concept and mood board (see 'Essential and creative planning', pages 10–23) in order to help you pinpoint the final look that you are after.

When deciding how best to display additional styling items in your lounge, there are a number of tricks for making your collections look their best. For immediate inspiration, study interiors magazines to see how professional stylists use a minimum number of objects for greatest impact. They do this by picking objects in colours that stand out from the rest of the décor (accent colours), for example, or by filling glass jars with a variety of objects such as buttons, fruit or flowers. Collections of at least three objects as a group have more impact, and repetition of objects can make even the ordinary appear extraordinary.

TIP: During a party situation, never attempt to find out what your beanbag is really made of — you will regret it for months as the static-filled polystyrene balls fly out in all directions!

Styling items for your lounge

- ▶ Books
- ▶ Vases
- ▶ Glassware
- ▶ Pictures, photos and artwork
- ▶ Objets trouvés – ordinary things that you find interesting
- ▶ Treasured things such as heirlooms or collected items
- ▶ Antiques
- ▶ Collections of objects – animal, mineral or vegetable
- ▶ Plants and flowers
- ▶ Decorative candles
- ▶ Lamps and side lights

Dining rooms

Over the years, people's attitudes to dining within their homes have changed dramatically. Gone are the days of grand, underused, austere dining rooms. Today, dining is a more informal affair, geared towards relaxation, fun and sociable times, and people's attitudes towards their dining areas reflect this. Dining space today is much more likely to be open plan, linked with another room and far less imposing. This means that dining rooms are often used for other purposes.

This chapter looks at both dedicated dining rooms and the more common, shared-space dining room – frequently a dining area within another room such as a kitchen or lounge. Whatever your type of space, it is necessary to create a functional area that has the ability to create atmosphere for your perfect evening in. It will, in essence, become an exercise in zoning a space, using the tools of interior design (furniture, lighting, colours, texture and accessories) to create something special.

Finally, remember that your dining area is likely to be used in different ways at different times of the day so flexibility through lighting and furniture is something that is worth remembering to allow you to get the most from your space.

Concepts and ideas When considering the concept for your dining area, think about the experience of dining and what you are looking to create. Does your image come from a film, a travelling experience or from your favourite restaurant? Whatever it is, consider the sensual pleasures of dining, and seek to enhance this in your interior style.

One of the most exciting aspects of planning your dining space is that you have the opportunity to consider all the body's senses within the concept you are about to create:

▶ **Sight** – this will be affected not only by the colour of the walls but also by the lighting. Use dimmer switches and candles to create a centrepiece of your table, which will be the canvas for the presentation of your food.

▶ **Sound** – think about whether you want this to be lively or subdued. The addition of music can be a powerful way to alter the acoustic quality of your room to suit your mood and the atmosphere of your dinner party. Background music will fill in silences and hide those embarrassing slurps from your toothless great-aunt!

▶ **Touch** – this will be affected by your floor surface, table surface, crockery, cutlery and glassware, all of which can add to the luxury of the experience of dining. Your type of chairs will also dramatically affect the atmosphere of any eating experience – do you want to sink into a chair that you can sit in and talk for hours, or are you looking for a more austere experience with benches? Remember, fast-food chains think carefully about their seating, designing chairs to encourage the user to sit, but not be too comfortable for more than five minutes. So consider how long you wish your guests or fellow diners to be seated for.

▶ **Taste** – if you can't cook, get yourself a cookbook and learn some basic recipes. Cooking is a therapeutic and creative process that can be a great destressor at the end of a long day. The food you produce will provide the focus of your dining experience, which, if shared with the right people, will be an enjoyable and sociable experience – one based around pleasuring the body's senses.

> **TIP:** When it comes to planning your dining space, remember that the perfect dining room should be a sensual experience.

▶ **Smell** – the preparation and cooking of food inevitably create odours. The fresh smells of cooking are your first impressions of the dining experience, while the smell of last week's curry is a stomach-churning turn-off! Your dining area should provide a fresh canvas for the aromatic qualities of the meal ahead. Having plants in the room and making sure it is well aired is important, as opposed to the overuse of air fresheners and incense, which can overcomplicate the whole experience.

Lighting

The variety of functions and different atmospheres you may want to create in your dining area means the lighting of the space is crucial. What you may want at breakfast time will be different to what you need when you sit and work or read at your table, which will again be different to the light required for an intimate dining experience or dinner party. The key words are flexibility and atmosphere. Central to this you need to consider three lighting types – general lighting, task and decorative lighting. A combination of all three will allow you flexibility and a sense of occasion for your dining needs.

General lighting This is the ambient lighting that you need in the space to allow you to move around the table safely when carrying trays of glasses or hot plates of food. It can be achieved by using a series of evenly spaced halogen downlighters, surface mounted to the ceiling, or by using wall-mounted uplighters that reflect off the ceiling and around the room. The dining room is really one of the only occasions when a ceiling-mounted pendant light is also appropriate as it can hang down over the table, illuminating and creating an atmosphere at the visual focus of the room: the table.

Task lighting These are the lights directed predominantly at the central focus of the room – your table – where the main activity in the room is based. If fitted with a dimmer switch, these can also double up as general lights. In the case of dining rooms, your task light and your general light may well be one and the same.

A good idea for focusing on your table is to suspend pendant lights from the ceiling above it. These should be positioned approximately 70–100 cm (28–39 in) above the table top and should allow light to fall onto the surface of the table, the lampshade preventing direct glare from the bulb reaching the eyes of the diners. If your dining space is part of a larger area such as your kitchen or lounge, ceiling-mounted pendant lights that hang over your dining table and are fixed with dimmer switches can be a great way of creating a sense of intimacy in this separate space.

Decorative lighting These lights help dramatically in creating atmosphere in your dining area – particularly if you are looking for a sense of intimacy or romance. They can also help create a balanced sense of light across the room, preventing strong contrasts of light from straining the eyes.

In their simplest and often most effective form, decorative lights can be candles. The light given by a candle is dynamic and warm, evoking primeval experiences of warmth, fire

A variety of lights give this dining room intimacy and atmosphere whilst being generally well enough lit so that you can see what you're eating!

and nature. When used on the table with candlesticks, candles can be one of the most flattering and romantic forms of lighting. Other decorative lights could be fairy lights, shaded side lights on dimmer switches, low-wattage bulbs or wall-mounted downlighters lighting specific objects or artwork.

Walls

The wall surface that you choose to have in your dining room will say much about your lifestyle and design aspirations, and will play an important part in creating a relaxed atmosphere for eating.

Traditionally, dining rooms employed wall-coverings such as hardwearing wallpapers, dado rails and paints to resist the wear and tear on the walls. Today's harder-wearing surfaces mean you have a greater choice of wallpapers, paints or even bare plaster.

When considering colour, remember that the walls of your dining room will provide the backdrop for the food you serve so it's probably best to stick to natural shades – think of food like rich chocolates, sage greens or burgundy reds. Alternatively, you could opt for a lighter tonal range of colours that will give the room a calming, relaxing feel.

Remember that you can also choose an alternative wall finish such as brick, plaster, or wooden boards that will give your dining room a sense of character and individuality.

Flooring

Although all the flooring types can be used in the dining area, your final choice should depend largely on the type of wear you expect it to have to suffer.

For a space that will be used often, consider a hard surface, which will last and be easy to clean. If the room is used only occasionally, you could opt for carpets or rugs although these will be harder to clean and the thought of spilling food on the floor can make for an anxious dining experience. Carpet will also affect the acoustics and trap odours.

If your dining area is part of a larger room, altering the floor surface can be an additional way of zoning the area – allowing it to feel more like a space in its own right. You may want to think about positioning a relatively hardwearing but soft floor surface beneath your table – ideally one that is relatively easy to replace, such as sea grass or coir floor mats, or a whip-stitched rug.

There aren't really any restrictions on which flooring type to opt for, but try not to have too many hard surfaces as these will make the space echo and feel cold. Introduce sound absorbent materials on the floors (in the form of rugs), walls or as window dressings.

Storage and display Traditionally, the storage associated with a dining area is more decorative than functional – for example, dressers were opportunities to display fine china and glassware. In general, this display of wealth is now seen as outdated, but do use decorative displays in this very public space to say what you want about yourself. Think also about how this will add to the dining experience – personal photos, for example, will help give the room a more relaxed feel.

Storage pieces such as decorative shelving and sideboards can store books, ornaments, artwork and photos, and should be seen as an opportunity to add character and atmosphere to your dining area. This will prevent it feeling underused and surplus to the everyday activities of your home.

The items you have in your dining room can also help to give the space a less echoey feel, making it feel warmer and more hospitable to spend time in.

If your dining room is a separate room in the house, you can use your storage and display to make it feel like a living, vibrant part of the home. Flowers and plants in particular will help you here.

This dining room uses shelving to display books, pictures and objects, giving it a sense of interest, intelligence and character.

Furniture Your dining space is likely to be another social hub of your home and the furniture you have should reflect this. A well-designed dining area is a sociable space, that will bring relaxation, conversation, and a sense of ritual to one's life – something that the pace of modern life has so quickly disposed of.

Built in seating is a good idea to make the most of small spaces and can offer additional storage space beneath it.

Dining table Your dining table will undergo a variety of activities – from eating at and working on, to entertaining around and, if you choose it well, will become a discussion point in its own right. Even if you don't have a dedicated dining room, emphasis should be put on the choice of the table. There are a great variety on offer, from solid fixed-top or expanding tables for accommodating dinner parties to folding tables and even a well-thought out island unit, which can serve as your dining area. However, your choice of table will largely be dictated by money and space.

When planning the layout of your dining space, it's a good idea to draw out a plan (see

'Understanding your space', pages 13–17). Position the table so that you have at least 120 cm (47 in) around the edge to accommodate chairs and access. This will then allow you to choose the right shape, width and length for your dining table. In areas of very limited space, you can think about using one of two tricks:

▶ A wall-mounted flip-up table will allow you to have a table when necessary but give you space to move when it is not in use.

▶ A fixed table and built-in bench seating is an efficient form of dining table and chairs.

If you are really short of space, or your room has to incorporate other activities, you could look to buy a fold-up table and set of chairs. Clever contemporary designs now allow you to store a decent-sized table and up to four folding chairs within its frame. When folded down, it is only 30 cm wide and 80 cm long (12 x 32 in), so can easily be stored in a spare corner when not in use.

Table surfaces The table surface that you choose will have a dramatic effect on the style and look of your space. There are many surfaces to choose from, which can be added to with extra layers of tablecloths and place settings when you dress the table for meals, creating a beautiful, inviting space to eat at.

▶ **Solid wood** – this can come in a variety of colours and surface finishes. Solid wood has a natural grain and texture, which can give the dining experience a more rustic feel. One of the best advantages of a wooden table is that it will improve with age and any marks just add

to its character, although it can always be sanded down and given a new surface finish to refresh your dining room for years to come.

▶ **Glass** – being both visually and acoustically reflective, glass will give a harder and more austere, yet also slicker and highly designed look to your dining area. It is hardwearing and easy to clean.

▶ **Plastic laminates** – these come in a massive range of colours and textures, from wood effect and patterned to straightforward colours. Although hardwearing, they are susceptible to the effects of heat and hence have a limited life as they will deteriorate with age. They are cheap and easy to clean but unlikely to become a family heirloom!

▶ **Tiles** – reminiscent of summer holidays, tiled table surfaces can be as exciting and as contemporary as you want to make them. As a do-it-yourself project, tiling can be a great way to personalize your dining space, using any of the massive range of tiles on offer or even creating a mosaic tabletop with fragments of

Far left: This wonderful solid wood table gives this space a warm organic and sociable feeling with just a nod towards rustic sensibilities.

Left: This glass table has a more sophisticated urban look in a room that is zoned through the use of a soft floor rug.

Right: These folding chairs give this dining space a greater flexibility to either fit more people at the table, or to be folded away to make space for other functions.

assortments of tiles. The downsides are that you must grout between the tiles carefully to prevent food or crumbs being caught, and a tiled surface can be difficult to work on if your table is used for activities other than eating.

► **Metal** – this is a more unusual choice but hardwearing and easy to clean with a more durable sense about your dining experience. It can give your dining area a retro look (think American diners) or a bistro feel (think of round, Parisian-style café tables).

Table shape When choosing your ideal table, think carefully about its shape and how it might fit into your dining area:

► **Square** – good for small spaces and intimate dining, square tables can be limiting for large numbers.

► **Rectangular** – a rectangular table has the advantages of intimacy and the ability to accommodate a larger number of people. The table's length will add to the horizontal lines of a room.

► **Circular** – while appearing sociable because more people can have eye contact, circular tables are in reality the most limited in usage. They are great for the right number of people but provide less intimacy with a smaller group and are inflexible for accommodating larger numbers.

Chairs Your choice of chairs will again be determined by the style, experience and budget that you need to fulfil. The cheapest and simplest option could be a case of giving a new lease of life to second-hand chairs with a quick paint job and reupholstering the seats, or by creating simple slip-on fabric covers to go over the whole chair. You could buy new chairs – there are a massive range on offer on the high street – or even benches for rectangular tables if you are looking for a more communal sense of dining. Whatever your decision, consider whether you want your dining table to be a place where people sit, relax and talk, or just get a quick bite to eat.

If you are buying your table and chairs separately, make sure that the heights of each suit each other. Your chairs should be low enough to allow your legs beneath the table without them rubbing against the underside; your table should be at the right height when you are sitting at it for your forearms to be horizontal on the tabletop.

Soft furnishings and styling items Soft furnishings, styling and accessories are the final layer to be added to the decorative style of your dining area. They are the finishing touches that will create a sense of personality and individuality, and reflect your character and dining aspirations.

Table dressings These can be a great opportunity to create an instant change in your dining room. Tablecloths and napkins can allow you to enjoy a sense of occasion or atmosphere – think white linen tablecloths for a touch of quality, or red and white checked napkins for a fondue evening. As they are relatively cheap, you can have fun experimenting. Go for plain, chequed, or baroque swirls – if you don't like it then you can whip it off and try something else!

Tableware More permanent than your table dressings will be your choice of crockery. Again, there is a wide variety to pick from, but think, before you buy, about the way your food will be presented. Much of today's crockery tends to be over-decorated, and can detract from the food, so opt for simpler styles that will show all your hard work off. They will also co-ordinate better with other items such as cutlery, glassware, and serving dishes.

Curtains These can be important not only for creating privacy but also for giving a greater sense of warmth. Curtains can help reduce echoes and, in addition, are a relatively easy way of adding colour, texture and a sense of luxury to the room. But remember to fix your curtains to maximize any available views from your dining space during the daytime.

Candles There are many sizes, shapes and colours of candles on offer, so consider co-ordinating these with your table settings. Remember that tall candles shine light up onto the face and down onto the table, whilst tealights will shine light up but not onto the table – these are best used in greater numbers. Most homestores will offer a variety of candle holders from candelabras to glass holders that catch the light beautifully.

Plants and flowers The addition of plants and flowers to your dining area will give it a more dynamic, lived-in feel. They will also help to freshen the air and retain a touch of nature within the space.

This dining room has a grand sense of elegance and sophistication through a high level of ornate styling, use of tablecloths, table runners candles and mirrors. It may however feel too formal for many of us to feel comfortable in.

TIP: Styling your dining area using books, objects, sculptures and art pieces on the wall will add character and depth to the look of the space.

Home offices

Increasingly, our homes are coming under more and more pressure to incorporate new functions, and none are more evident than in the rise of the 'home office'. Whether it is so that your home can go on-line, your employer has decided to start 'hot desking' or even that you just need somewhere to store your bills and papers, it's likely that you now need a space to sit and work.

So, if you are going to have an office or workspace in the home, do you want it to look like the place where you go to work? It doesn't have to – it can be light, energetic, bright, invigorating, calming and designed to fit your needs. As ever, it will require a little thought and preplanning to consider your spatial, organizational, technological and stylistic needs before you go out and spend your money.

Concepts and planning The question is how much space do you need, and where are you going to find it in your home? To reduce the impact of an office in your home, you may want to find or create a space that offers a level of privacy – one that will hide your private business affairs, or one that simply reduces the visual clutter of cables and office equipment in the home.

While you may start out working at your kitchen table, this will inevitably impact on your domestic life and a more permanent solution needs to be found in your home. There are three main areas that you could look at:

▶ If you have the space, you could look towards dedicating a complete room to the creation of a home office.

▶ You could double up the function of a room such as a guest bedroom.

▶ If you don't have the luxury of space, you could look to zone an area within an existing room to store your computer, files and books.

The first solution of dedicating a complete room to an office means that you can shut yourself and your business affairs away from prying eyes and interruptions, to allow yourself some peace and quiet to concentrate. If you do have the space this is clearly going to be the best option, allowing you to lay out your work and to use the room undisturbed as a permanent workspace. However, you should also consider whether your home office will have an impact on other members of the house – for example, the sound of a chair on castors rolling over the floor and creating noise in the room below.

With the second scenario, which involves doubling up the function of a spare bedroom, it's important to remember that the room will have to function effectively for two quite contrasting activities. As a workspace it will need sufficient storage, space for a computer and additional peripherals and an invigorating feel to it. As a guest bedroom, however, you need to make sure that your guests are comfortable and not made to feel as if they are encroaching on your private business affairs. Hence, ensuring confidential material can be locked away is important. You should aim to achieve a balance by creating a calm, relaxing and welcoming atmosphere in the room that encourages both work and sleep.

Above: This efficient home office makes the most of a small nook to create a pleasingly self-contained private area.

Right: Home offices in the bedroom mean that you can never get away from your work; your bedroom should be an escape.

Far right: A better solution is to give your computer and work space a dedicated cabinet that can be closed up and look beautiful when not in use.

TIPS:

Remember that your office needs to be properly served by sufficient electric sockets for all your office equipment and telephone sockets to facilitate vocal and fax communication and internet access. Be careful not to overload sockets as this can lead to electrical failures and fires.

Remember the environmental issues that affect your workspace – save energy by turning off electrical equipment at night, recycle paper and used printer cartridges (see 'Greener homes', pages 238–45 for more information).

Try not to confuse the function of spaces in your home. An office in your bedroom will prevent you from getting away from your work – try to position it out of sight or in an area with a similar activity level.

The third option relies on zoning, when you separate two or more areas in an existing room to accommodate different functions. This can be as simple as creating a built-in cupboard to house all your business affairs or using changes in materials, wall colour, light or elements of furniture to define the different areas and activities.

Whatever your space, you will want your work area to be functional, well organized, efficient, bright, enlivening and, most of all, a pleasure in which to sit down and work. It's the opportunity to create a personalized workspace – one that will allow your working life and the needs for technology to coexist in harmony with your personal domestic life.

Lighting

Lighting Lighting can dramatically influence your energy and attention span. No room in the house demonstrates this better than your home office. Due to the level of concentration and visual focus needed for detailed work or reading, it's important to attain a balanced level of lighting to prevent additional strain on your eyes. For this reason, you must consider the general lighting levels in the room and task lights to illuminate areas of specific activity.

Natural light This will dramatically affect your energy levels within your workspace and should be encouraged for this reason as well as the fact that maximizing on it will reduce your office energy use and therefore your electricity bills. However, using this dynamic lighting source can also present problems due to the high levels of glare and the reflections it creates, which can make staring at your monitor difficult.

To counteract this, it's a good idea to consider a flexible window covering that enables you to control the amount of natural light that enters the space. One of the best options is a Venetian blind as you can adjust the height and opening aperture to affect the incoming light very efficiently. If this is too harsh an option, you could also consider a roller or Roman blind, both of which offer a level of flexibility with minimal visual impact (see 'Window dressings', pages 94–99).

General lighting It is important to get an even spread of light across your work area. This may be best carried out using a number of ceiling-mounted lights. However, this can produce glare, which tires the eyes so another good option is to use multiple uplighters to reflect light evenly across the ceiling. It can also be good to fit dimmer switches to control the level of lighting at all times of the day. Another favourite is to use fluorescent strip lights. Although these can have an office or industrial feel, recent technological developments mean they are now more suitable for domestic use as they flicker less and have a very long life span.

One thing to consider with your office lighting is whether you will be doing any creative or visual work involving colour as colours can be surprisingly altered under different types of bulb. Standard tungsten bulbs have a yellowy quality, while fluorescent strip tubes appear green and halogen bulbs are probably the nearest to normal daylight. For the seriously colour-aware, you can buy daylight-correction bulbs, which simulate the colour rendering of natural light, from most good art supply stores and lighting shops.

Task lighting To achieve a balance between the general lighting in a room and a work area such as your desk, where you may be reading or using the computer, it is important to use specific task lights. These come in a variety of forms that will also let you personalize the style of your workspace and can be anything from an angle-poise lamp to mini fluorescent strip tubes. When choosing a task light for your desk, make sure that it has a stable base with a switch. The main light source should be adjustable and sit at least 30 cm (12 in) above the desktop. It's also a good idea to buy one with a shade of some sort to prevent glare going directly into your eyes when you are working. Task lights can also help to balance the lighting levels in a room – for instance, lighting up the dark area behind your monitor to counteract the brightness of your screen, thereby reducing eye strain.

This compact and functional work area is well served by its tabletop task lighting.

This workspace has good, well planned, easy to reach wall storage and uses colour to inject a sense of energy.

Walls Again, you have a great opportunity in your home office to personalize your space. You can create whatever mood or atmosphere you want – light and airy, funky and retro, a Zen area of calm or a museum piece full of the things that inspire you. Depending on the sort of work you intend to carry out, you may want to limit the amount of visual detail with which you adorn your office walls. It could be inappropriate to use heavily patterned wallpapers, for example, or other excessive details which may interfere with the need for a clear head. Alternatively, limit them to walls you are not directly facing when working.

It can clearly be a good idea to decorate your workspace in a way that suggests energy, excitement, enthusiasm, light and space. However, this can be in opposition with the function of your room if it doubles up as a spare bedroom – when it should be calm and welcoming for guests. If this is the case, you may want to think more carefully about zoning your desk space. A good idea is to paint the walls of the room a calm, restful colour but to paint the inside of your storage cupboards with bright, energetic colours so that when you open them there will be a feeling of your workspace bursting into life.

Flooring Although the flooring in your home office will largely be to your personal taste, consider a few practicalities before you decide to plump for a fluffy carpet! From a functional point of view, remember that computers and fax machines have fans that circulate air around their systems. Although you can vacuum regularly, it is inevitable that hairs and dust will get sucked into your equipment. A cleaner and more dust-free flooring surface than carpet may therefore be better – for example, rubber, stone, tiles, wood, laminates/engineered floors and linoleum or vinyl (see 'Flooring', pages 70–85 for more information).

While these surfaces are easier to keep clean, they are also much more efficient if you enjoy zooming around on your wheelie chair… However, racing around your home office may disturb others in the home or on the floor below as harder floor surfaces tend to conduct sounds throughout the building. If you are thinking about putting your home office where there may be bedrooms below, you might consider creating an acoustic barrier between the storeys as noise pollution between neighbouring spaces can be unbearable. One of the easiest and cheapest ways of doing this is to fit an acoustic underlay. This layer of high-grade felt and rubber reduces impact noise through the floor and can be laid beneath carpet, wood and laminate-type floorings. For more information, talk to a flooring specialist.

The wooden floor in this office will allow the wheelie chair to glide around effortlessly making daily use of this space much easier – and more fun!

Storage elements When thinking about storage in your home office, remember that you will need to access some things more frequently than others and that you should try to leave a certain amount of room for personalization so that your office doesn't become a purely functional space.

The important thing to remember about storage for your home office is that you don't really want your business affairs to be on display in your home space. Visual clutter of this kind can increase stress levels and it is sometimes better to be able to put your work away and concentrate on your home life. For this reason, it is a good idea to consider storage elements that you can close, like built-in units, cupboards or even filing cabinets. A physical distinction should be made between your work life and your private life.

▸ **Items to be accessible/on display** – telephone, books, personal objects, photographs, knick-knacks, plants, stereo, noticeboard

▸ **Items in daily use that you may or may not want on display** – stationery (pens, paper, envelopes, stamps), stapler, hole punch, paper clips, dictionary, diary, telephone directories, current subscriptions/magazines, CDs/radio, office toys, paperwork (in/out trays), computer/printer/scanner, fax machine

▸ **Items used weekly** – files for current projects, bills, etc.

▸ **Items used infrequently and not for display** – spare paper, printer ink, etc.

Filing cabinets/metal cupboards/lockers/drawer units These items are sometimes undervalued, but can, in the eyes of the organized, be the storage equivalent of domestic bliss. Although they might appear plain and simple, they can be marvellously practical, allowing you to keep an enormous number of papers and files in clearly labelled order. Not only that, they can be much more versatile in the way they look if you are willing to put a bit of imagination into it. You can spray them, strip them down to the bare metal and varnish them, or cover them with reclaimed timber, pad them with material, wallpaper them, or use them with magnets as metallic noticeboards.

Shelving Open or covered shelves are the obvious choice for quick and easy storage and there's a variety of options. Buy flat-packed shelves from furniture stores, or opt for the classic-style perforated metal shelving for versatility. You can fix vertical metal rods to the wall, into which you fit hooked brackets or simply drill holes for individual shelves with their own brackets.

If you go for a freestanding unit, make sure the shelves are properly cross-braced, which means they have a diagonal cross-member to stop them falling sideways. It's also a good idea to fix the top of the back of the unit to the wall to prevent them falling forwards.

For wall-mounted brackets, make sure you have the correct fixings for the type of wall to which you are fitting them. Solid masonry walls provide a good solid surface to fix brackets using screws and wall plugs. With plasterboard partition walls, which sound hollow when you knock them, you will have to be more careful, and either screw into the vertical wooden supports that are inside the wall or use screws and special plasterboard fixings. Either way, be sure throughout the lives of your shelves that you don't fill them with too many heavy objects – if you do and they come down, you're going to have one unbelievable mess on your hands that's really only funny much later on!

Built-in storage For the most efficient use of space, you cannot beat a purpose-made, built-in cupboard that will neatly house all your files, stationery and electronic equipment, and that has doors or screens that you can close when not in use. The best way to approach this is to have a clear idea on paper as to exactly what it is that you need to store and where you want to site it. The unit will also need to include a means of dealing with your electrical requirements, perhaps by including holes in the back through which you can run your cables. Once you have your plan, contact a local carpenter or furniture maker for a quote (see 'Employing contractors', pages 234–7).

Furniture With the increasing rise of repetitive strain injury (RSI), it is becoming more evident that the way in which we operate at work is crucial for our health and wellbeing. Hence, the ergonomics of your workspace – your posture and means of operating around your desk – are a prime consideration when choosing your furniture if you are to spend any longer than one hour at your desk every day. All good furniture stores now have areas dedicated to the home office and it is worth investing in adjustable furniture that will suit you and your family's needs. Each aspect of office furniture will need some consideration.

Correct body posture For comfort and health while at work you must be aware of the optimum working position of your body and the design of your workstation. Contrary to the image promoted by laptop computer adverts, being free of your desk does not mean you can work just anywhere. Within a very short period of time of working in your favourite armchair, for example, you will realize that having the wrong posture at work really will be a pain in the neck.

There are a few basic rules when it comes to your body posture, so ensure that your:

▶ Head looks straight forward to your computer screen, with your eyes level with the top half of it. You should have a maximum of 15 per cent decrease in angle when looking towards the screen.

▶ Shoulders are relaxed
▶ Upper arms drop vertically down by your sides with your forearms horizontal while working at the computer keyboard
▶ Back is straight with adequate support at belt level
▶ Knees are at right angles to the ground and clear of the underside of your desk
▶ Feet are not obstructed but flat on the floor

It is clearly impossible for the height of a desk to be right for an adult and, at the same time, right for a child, so adjustable furniture is essential if your workspace is going to accommodate more than one person. Even if it is only for your private rather than business use, properly designed furniture will really take the strain out of working at home.

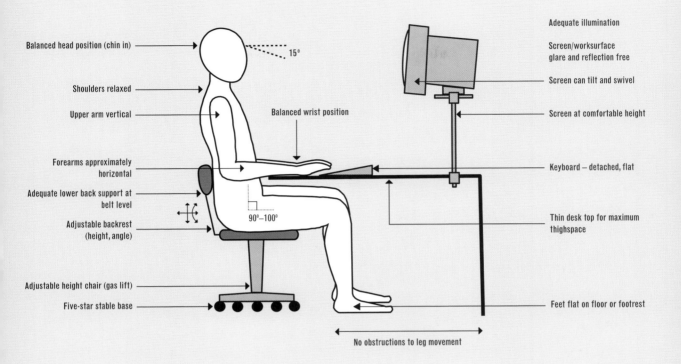

Balanced head position (chin in)

15°

Shoulders relaxed

Upper arm vertical

Balanced wrist position

Forearms approximately horizontal

Adequate lower back support at belt level

Adjustable backrest (height, angle)

90°–100°

Adjustable height chair (gas lift)

Five-star stable base

No obstructions to leg movement

Adequate illumination

Screen/worksurface glare and reflection free

Screen can tilt and swivel

Screen at comfortable height

Keyboard – detached, flat

Thin desk top for maximum thighspace

Feet flat on floor or footrest

Working requirements to help you achieve the correct body posture

▶ Your desk should …

Provide plenty of layout space for documents and
   computer equipment

Have a document holder for ease of use while typing

Not be highly reflective – to reduce glare

Be high enough so that the user's legs do not scrape
   its underside

▶ Your chair should …

Be stable and not rock around

Support the lower back and, if possible, the forearms with
   arm rests

Have an adjustable back – both angle of tilt and height

Have a height-adjustable seat

▶ Your monitor should …

Have a base that swivels so you can tilt it

Be on a stand or base so that your head is at the right
angle and your eyes are level with the top half of the
computer screen

Have brightness and contrast controls that can be
   adjusted to prevent eye strain

Be able to swivel easily

▶ Your keyboard should …

Be separate from your screen – get an additional keyboard
   if you work from a laptop for any length of time,
   otherwise your head will always be angled downwards

Be able to tilt

Have enough desk space in front of it to adequately
   support your wrists and forearms

Whilst this computer area makes a good use of space, poor seating will result in it being uncomfortable.

Desk It's important to consider the desktop technology that you are going to need at your fingertips. You must consider the depth of your computer monitor, the size and shape of the keyboard and, in addition, where the main body of the computer will sit if you have a tower system, bearing in mind that computer cables are often of limited length and their prolific number can mean that it is good to think about a cable management system, similar to the one you have in your lounge (see page 180). You might also consider labelling each plug with the appliance name to make

sure that you don't pull out the wrong one! As well as what you will need on your desk in front of you, it is often useful to have additional space for stationery, books, papers and files that you will need open as you sit and work.

A standard straight desk may be sufficient, but it is often more convenient from an ergonomic point of view to sit at an L-shaped arrangement of worksurfaces so that additional pieces of equipment such as telephone, fax machine and printer can be at arm's length without the need for gymnastic stretching. In addition, the height of your desk is clearly an important issue in relation to the chair that you use at it (see box, page 211).

If you have an unusual sized or shaped niche that you wish to fit your worksurface into, then you could buy the legs and a table-top separately and cut the top to fit.

Seating It's really worth spending as much as you can on a good office chair, particularly if you are going to be spending any length of time in it. Remember, go for function first, rather than simply the look. Adjustability is the key to buying a chair that is appropriate for the home office. You must make sure that your body is properly supported when working at your desk and you should be able to have your feet flat on the floor by adjusting the height of the chair seat. It's up to you whether you want a chair on castors or not.

One of the great benefits of working at home is that you are not restricted to other people's methods and space allocation. So it is a great idea to have alternative forms of seating in your home office area. This could be as simple as having beanbags and floor cushions to lounge around on while taking a break or as sophisticated as a leather armchair to sit comfortably in when reading books, documents, or even your favourite magazine while other people are thinking you're working hard. It's a great way of personalizing your space and creating a sense of harmony within your working life.

Soft furnishings In an office space that could well be filled with hard surfaces, such as floors, walls and cupboard doors, you should really think about the layering of soft furnishings for a number of reasons:

▶ Acoustically, they soften the sound of the room, preventing it from sounding acoustically live or echoey, like a bathroom, when you are on the phone.

▶ They allow you to personalize and decorate the area, which is necessary for a happy and enjoyable workspace.

▶ They increase the comfort of the space, again, making it more enjoyable to be in.

▶ They make the atmosphere more presentable for any business meetings you may have.

Soft furnishings in a home office may well include a rug for the floor, cushions on the chairs, throws over a reading chair and curtains or blinds to insulate the room at night or to prevent sunlight streaming into the room and creating glare. The soft furnishings in your room can provide necessary visual texture to enrich the look of the space and can be easily changed from season to season depending on your evolving taste.

A comfortable armchair and side light make this corner a pleasure to sit and read in.

Corridors and hallways

As with meeting people, first impressions of your home will count. Your front door and hallway are the first areas that any visitor to the house will experience. Even more important than that, they are the first and last place that you will see every day on entering or leaving the house, so it is important that they reflect a little bit of who you are and how you want to be. Beyond this, your hallway and corridors are largely functional spaces – areas to pass through between rooms and their different atmospheres. Often, they are restricted in size so there is little additional room for personalization and furniture. Thinking carefully about these areas, however, will mean that they become more than just a dumping ground but something to feel proud of.

Remember that the hallway and corridors of your home are the arteries of your house. An old, sagging, creaking staircase can really give a tired feeling to your home, so think about revitalizing it. Fix any wonky creaking stairs, strip the layers of paint from the balustrade and hand rail, fit a new carpet, fill in dents and cracks in the wall, fit some new lights and your house will start to feel re-energized from its core. Remember that you can always close a door to a room but your hallway will be there every time you move through your home so it is important to make it feel like a place in its own right.

Concepts As areas of great activity, entrances and corridors suffer from a high level of wear and tear, so from the outset it is a good idea to design this space to take the knocks and bashes that everyday life will throw at it. In addition to this, it will also be a very public space, allowing you to say a little bit about yourself as you welcome guests into your home. You may therefore want your entrance and corridor to feel bright, welcoming and energetic, and be free of clutter.

From another point of view, your corridors and hallway are the spaces that link together the separate rooms in your home. This means you could create a neutral link between the various styles of the rooms, producing a sense of harmony from room to room. Alternatively, you could regard the corridors and hallway as a space in which you spend little time and so feel more comfortable about using stronger, bolder colours for a much more dynamic feel. You could achieve this by using a more graphic style such as vertical stripes, horizontal bands or simply blocks of colour.

Both this hallway and stair landing have character and identity and link the rooms of the home neatly together.

Lighting

Being functional areas used mainly for circulation, entrances and corridors require good and clear lighting. Ideally, you need to think about general ambient light and occasional task lighting. Atmospheric lighting, although nice, is less important here. From a safety aspect, it is essential that the stairs and obstructions are clearly visible as these can easily trip people up. As hall lights are often left on for long periods of time, you could consider using energy saving light bulbs to save you money, or fit timer switches so that the lights are only on when you actually need them to be.

Windows It is a good idea to make maximum use of any windows that you have in your hallway. You can do this by positioning mirrors close to them, taking care not to obscure them with oversized curtains or simply by painting the window surrounds white to reflect the maximum amount of light into the space. If you do need to screen the window for privacy reasons, there are a wide variety of sheer fabrics to choose from, which let light filter in and screen views. Alternatively, you can apply a glass etch spray or frosted-glass effect film to the window to give total obscuration (see 'Retaining privacy', pages 40–41). If your hall window backs onto an unsightly view, you could also think about using textured obscured glass as the undulations in the surface can catch the light and bounce it into the space.

General lighting You will need good, even ambient lights throughout the length of your hallway, but if you want to be kinder to your eyes in the middle of the night, these can be fitted with dimmer switches. The choice of light is entirely up to you – ceiling-mounted downlighters, halogen spotlights or pendant lights would all be appropriate. It's a good idea to coordinate the lighting throughout all the corridors in your house to give a cohesive look.

Task lighting Although there might be limited opportunity for task lights, you can create a really stunning look up your stairs by using wall-mounted, recessed stair lights. You may need three or four to light a whole staircase but they do give a well-thought out, professional look to the interior of your home. They are relatively cheap to buy but the labour of chasing the cables into the walls and fitting the units can make them expensive. The only other place in which you may need task lights is by a mirror near the front door, where you might check your appearance before leaving the house.

Accent and decorative lighting Although entrance hallways and corridors are largely functional, it can be a lovely welcome home to see a soft warm light glowing in your hallway. This could be a lamp on a sideboard or hall table, or a wall-mounted light. The latter could double as an accent light, highlighting a specific feature or artwork displayed in the hall.

These stair lights are a good designer detail that will be atmospheric and highly functional.

TIPS:

Think about positioning a mirror in the hallway. This can have the effect of bouncing light in through the door or a window and gives you the chance to check your appearance before you leave the house.

Fit an exterior porch light to welcome guests and to allow identification of callers through your door spyhole at night.

TIPS:

Artwork in the hallway can brighten the area.

A noticeboard in the hallway can be a good idea, reminding you of things to do before leaving the house or while you are out.

The pictures on the wall give this hallway character and a sense of rhythm that breaks up its length.

Walls

The high level of activity and movement in entrances and corridors means that walls inevitably take more of a battering here than in other areas of the house. It's therefore a good idea to use hardwearing finishes or at least those that are easily maintained, such as paint. Decorative and delicate wallpapers should really be avoided. Traditionally, hallway walls had dado rails with thick textured wallpaper and high skirting boards to prevent damage, but as modern paints are now tougher and easier to maintain, these architectural features are not strictly necessary, allowing you to be freer with the look of your hallway.

It may seem like common sense, but ideally your hallway should be the last place that you decorate for the very simple reason that in installing the fixtures and fittings throughout the rest of the house, everything has to pass through the hallway. Inevitably, this is going to create damage to the walls, no matter how careful you are.

To break up the feel of a lengthy corridor, a simple trick is to display pictures or objects dotted along the walls to alter the sense of perspective created by the corridor. This can either be in a series of small arrangements or more uniformly along its length. A similar trick is to make clever use of mirrors to increase the sense of depth within a dead-end space. Mirrors not only reflect light and increase the sense of space but can also be used to double the impact of displays positioned in front of them – for example, arrangements of flowers or plants will appear fuller and sculptures more three-dimensional.

Flooring

The flooring in your entrance and corridors should be hardwearing and relatively easy to clean to cope with the high level of activity and the dirt walked in from outside. A good compromise between practicality and warmth is to have a hard floor and supplement it with a hallway runner or rug. This will make the space feel welcoming and stop it sounding too echoey. If you are going to have a rug in the hall, make sure you use an anti-slip rubber underlay to prevent it slipping.

If you are considering fitting a new floor on top of the existing one, remember that the floor height will now be different from other rooms, and that the first step of the stairs will be smaller, which may be a trip hazard. It is a good idea to fix a metal strip across thresholds to highlight this change in level and you may need to get your doors planed down so they still open.

This natural covering on the stairs will be hard wearing and soften the noise of footsteps as people go up and down them.

Appropriate flooring for hallways

- **Solid wood/engineered floor** Both of these are a good solid choice for hallways.
- **Laminate floor** This is a cheap and effective option but remember that excess water – possibly from a pair of boots – can make the flooring swell and warp out of shape.
- **Painted/varnished wooden floorboards** This is the cheapest solution but the finish will need reapplying every 12–18 months, depending on the level of foot traffic across the floor.
- **Stone floor** This type of flooring is easy to clean and maintain but may need the addition of a rug or runner for visual warmth.
- **Floor tiles** Tiles are easy to clean but the grout lines can attract and hold dirt.
- **Rubber floor** This is hardwearing but does mark easily and so needs cleaning frequently.
- **Carpet** Make sure you buy a very hardwearing type.

Storage You may need to find storage space in your hallway or corridor for shoes and boots, coats, umbrellas, a recycling area (cans, bottles, plastics, card and paper) and meter boxes, yet there is nothing more unsightly than an entrance to a home cluttered with items like shoes and stacks of coats. In the overall design of your home, try to find somewhere conveniently near your front door that will allow you to store these items without them being the first thing that you see. This could be a hallway cupboard but you could also use a series of hooks and shoe shelves to store clutter in one place and off the ground. Try to keep unworn coats in cupboards and not stored in the hallway, blocking access and circulation around your home.

This simple storage solution can hide shoes, keys and letters, and still be used to style the hallway to give it some character.

It's a good idea to have somewhere to store your keys as you walk in through the front door. A key rack, hooks or drawer of some type can save you that frantic searching for keys whenever you leave the house. This should be situated out of sight of the open door and in a place that prevents access to them by thieves who could use the letter box to reach them. (While we're talking about keys, call on somebody you trust right now and arrange to leave your spare keys with them, should you ever get locked out or have your bag stolen — honestly, you'll thank me for this one day!)

Furniture and fittings

Hallways and corridors are dynamic, practical areas, and as such, any items you choose to go in them will need to have a functional quality – the trick is to combine this with making the space as beautiful as possible. making the right choices will help you to create a characterful first impression of your home.

The front door Unless you have a strong idea of something different, your front door should ideally match the architectural style of the property. The best way to gauge this is to look at other houses in the street and see what appears to be the norm. If you feel that yours looks out of place, contact a door manufacturer to buy an appropriate one (take a photo of some neighbouring doors to show them what you want) or, if you live in a period property, visit a salvage yard to find one to match. When buying a door, it's important to remember that it is much easier to buy a bigger door and cut it down to size rather than buy a smaller one and try to add to its width or height, which also makes it less secure.

The right door furniture will also have a dramatic effect on the look of the entrance to your property. Ideally, choose the appropriate letter box, door handle and door knocker for the style of door. However, simple it is,

This coordinated scheme ties in the colour of the front door with the character of the interior style.

undecorated, contemporary door furniture can also provide a stylish look when blended with a period-style door.

From a security point of view, your letter box should have a back cover plate to stop prying eyes seeing past the front door and to help prevent draughts. You should have a strong mortise lock that conforms to a recognized

standard (in the UK this will be BS 3621) in addition to a latch lock, which does not provide sufficient security on its own – good locks will be required to satisfy your insurance company. An intercom or video-entry phone allows an initial conversation without the risk of opening the front door to a stranger. Similarly, a spyhole allows you to view the caller before opening the door although its vision can be deceptive. Fitting a security chain will prevent someone trying to gain entry but can be breached by a determined intruder, so find out who is at the door first. If your front door has glass panels, make sure they are textured, opaque or obscured.

Do consider the entrance to your home as part of the overall design. If you have a dedicated path with flower beds or pots, plant flowers to complement the approach to your home. The colour of your front door can also reflect the interior design style of your hallway.

Stairs These are dynamic places and foot traffic on the stairs tends to create a lot of noise, which, if you share a house with other people, can be disturbing. It is therefore a good idea to fit a runner in the form of carpet or matting up the entire length of your stairs. This will not only deaden the noise from people running up and down them, but also makes them a little softer, should someone happen to fall down stairs.

From a safety point of view, fix any loose floorboards before fitting a stair carpet or runner. Once a floorboard has come loose, it will only get worse the more it is used and it is dangerous for anybody unaware of it. Equally, while it may be a cool style statement to do away with the hand rail, this can be unsafe, particularly for the young and the elderly.

To give your hallway and staircase a new lease of life, an exciting but potentially costly project is to fit a contemporary hand rail and balustrade. This can be made from a variety of materials, for example structural glass, aluminium, wood or welded steel. Approach at least two manufacturers for quotes as prices can vary massively.

Extra furniture Many hallways and corridors have small, unused areas that can be utilized to add character and depth to the circulation spaces of your home. If big enough, they can take a piece of furniture such as a chair, sideboard or display plinth, which can be used for temporary storage of mail and keys, or for a display of some sort – artwork, personal photos, sculptural elements or plants – allowing you to add a personal touch to the space and to say something about yourself to the people who enter your home. Alternatively, think about using display shelves but make sure they are small enough so as not to obstruct movement through the area.

Be very careful about the dimensions of any piece of furniture within hallways or corridors as a circulation space less than 70 cm (28 in) wide will invariably make an area feel too cramped. A good idea may be to buy a purpose made, second hand or antique console table as these tend to be fairly narrow so won't obstruct the path through the hallway, but are just big enough for some flowers or a plant, a side lamp and some keys.

Although furniture can be a useful feature to have in your entranceway, make sure it doesn't just become a dumping ground for unsorted mail, coats, books and bags. Horizontal surfaces do have a tendency to attract surplus bits and pieces, and it is sometimes important to look afresh at your hallway and see if it is really saying something about you that is positive.

Doormat It might sound obvious but a doormat is the easiest way of preventing unwanted dust and grime from the street from dirtying your home. Ideally, an external and an internal doormat will stop dust going further but for the neatest solution, you can fit a coir doormat permanently to the floor inside the door.

Say something about yourself in your hallway using side tables, and what ever takes your fancy... First impressions always count!

Meter box Some houses have their meter boxes for water, gas and electricity somewhere in the hallway. These can be extremely unsightly and it is best to think of ways to hide them. Ideally, this involves installing a hinged cupboard that allows for occasional access. If the meter box is in a prominent position, it can be a good idea to fit a push-to-open catch to the door of the cupboard. This means that you don't need a door handle, which can accentuate the cupboard needlessly.

The
Extras

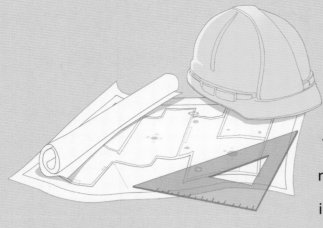

If you are considering more than just a simple restyling or redecoration of your home, it is inevitable that at some stage you will need to consult professionals to carry out specific tasks that are clearly out of your technical experience. In addition, many larger works will need official legal permission, particularly if they affect the external look of your property, or in any way affect the safety and efficiency of your home. This will open up a whole new area of home improvement, and you must understand the correct processes and procedures before spending your hard earned money.

Taking it further

Calling in professionals

While tackling the do-it-yourself projects and interior design of your home can be rewarding, you will inevitably come to a task that your skills cannot cover. At this point you need the services of a trained, qualified and experienced professional to explain the process and carry out the job in hand. This professional advice could cover anything from a basic homebuyer's survey or architectural design to plumbing and electrics. It is important that you understand what these professionals can do for you and how best to approach them in order for them to understand your needs and give you exactly what you want at a price that suits your budget. The more information you can give them, the better the service you will receive back. Hiring professionals need not be costly and they will invariably carry out complicated tasks where their experience will prove invaluable.

Surveyors It is a surveyor's job to inspect a property and highlight the various visible defects. Although a surveyor's report can prove to be an upsetting read – detailing everything from peeling paint to leaky gutters – it's essential that you know what state a property is in before you buy it. You will undoubtedly be asked by your mortgage company to undertake a survey of the property you are about to buy. They will ask you to undertake either a Homebuyer's Report or a Full Structural Survey of the property. The former is a general inspection of the property listing all its basic defects. The latter includes

information in greater detail and will give you a much clearer picture as to the property's existing state. For peace of mind, this is the safer option.

While a surveyor will endeavour to highlight all visible defects in their report, it will be almost impossible for them to report on those areas that cannot be seen, such as joists and beams and the flooring beneath carpets, so it is still possible for problems to occur in areas that have not been inspected. Once the report has been written, you must study it to understand the various defects and the urgency with which they must be fixed. Some may be as simple as replacing a rotten window frame or scraping off peeling paint, but others may be more complex – for example, cracked plaster, which could suggest structural problems, subsidence and the possibility of damp.

The best way to find yourself a surveyor in the UK is by contacting the Royal Institute of Chartered Surveyors. Alternatively, you could try contacting a local estate agent, who will have regular contact with surveyors operating on a domestic scale in your area. It's likely that they will be familiar with your type of property and the sort of issues that may occur.

Architects If you are planning major changes to your home, which include those to the layout or its structure, it is worthwhile employing an architect to lead you through part or all of the process. An architect can help you with a variety of elements, such as:
► Creating a design
► Drawing up plans and elevations
► Applying for planning permission

- Submitting Building Control applications
- Finding a builder and sorting out a contract with them
- Putting together specifications and scope of works for your builder
- Overseeing the work on-site and acting between the parties, bringing everyone together for a successful scheme

Initially, it's worth meeting two or three architects to see how you feel about them and to discuss your ideas. It will help if you have images to show them of the sort of design you are after. You should also have an idea of your intended start and completion dates, and the sort of money you are looking to spend. At your initial meeting with the architects, they will advise you on some of these points and it's also useful if you can see their portfolio of previous work. The best ways to find an architect are by contacting the Royal Institute of British Architects (in the UK) by looking at design magazines or via word of mouth.

Once you've selected your architect, they will send you a letter of appointment laying out their terms and conditions of employment, the services they will provide, a rough scope of works for your project, an outline schedule for the works and their preferred methods of payment. It's important when working with professionals like architects that you uphold your part of the contract with them and act in a professional manner. Having your home renovated and redesigned can be a stressful process; your architect will be there to help you through it and to mediate between yourself and the contractors and specialists working on the project. It's important to follow their requests in order to achieve a successful result.

Interior designers For help and advice on your interiors or for projects that may require only minor structural work but a high level of interior design specification, contact an interior designer. They will help you with a variety of elements to guide you through the interior design process – that is, if you haven't already learnt it all from this book or just don't have the time to do it yourself! An interior designer will help you with:
- The design process – looking for inspiration, concepts, colours and ideas
- The circulation of your space – affected by walls, screens and furniture
- The specification of fixtures, fittings and finishes
- The lighting design
- Storage
- Finding a contractor to carry out the work
- Overseeing the work on-site

Again, the clearer your picture of what you want, the more the designer will be able to create the look you are after within the spatial and financial constraints of the project. Go through magazines, pick out images, take photographs and put together a mood board (see 'Creating a mood board', pages 20–21) of what you are after before approaching two or three designers to consider the project.

Like an architect, an interior designer will send you a letter of appointment outlining various elements of the project such as the scope of works, the services they will carry out for you, a time schedule and their preferred methods of payment. Remember that having the interior of your home designed can be an emotional and stressful ordeal so try to work with your interior designer in as professional a manner as possible.

To find an interior designer you could contact the Chartered Society of Designers, look through your local telephone directory or, ideally, locate one via word of mouth or by looking at magazine articles. Although the Chartered Society of Designers only has, at present, a database of UK based designers, you will find that other countries have organisations that provide the same service.

Structural engineers If you wish to carry out a structural modification to your property it is essential that you contact a structural engineer before carrying out any job that may have structural implications on your building. Failure to do so could lead to catastrophic consequences so it is well worth paying out a relatively small sum for the advice of a structural engineer as opposed to the possible reconstruction costs of your entire house and possibly your neighbour's too!

A structural engineer can advise you on removing a wall to open up space, removing a chimney, installing bigger doors or creating new openings in the external fabric of your property. Initially, you will need a structural engineer to inspect the property to assess its current structural state and then to work out the details of any structural calculations that may be needed for building control

submissions and also in order for your builder to carry out the work safely and professionally. You will need to discuss what you want and the end effect you wish to create. Inevitably, much of the work that the structural engineer will do for you will be covered over, so it's important for you to know how the final effect you are trying to achieve will look. You may wish to coordinate the work of your architect with that of the structural engineer in order to create a complete and well-thought out scheme.

The best way to contact a structural engineer in the UK is through the Institution of Structural Engineers (www.istructe.org.uk) which will advise you on who to contact in your local area. Each country will have a similar organisation, so if you are outside the UK, you should still be able to find a registered engineer.

Official permissions

Generally, when carrying out larger projects on your home you will need to contact your local authority to seek advice and permission on the viability of your intended scheme. There are two types of official permission and they should be contacted separately before you start any major work that affects the state of your property. They are:

▶ Building Regulations – these relate to the safety, quality and energy efficiency of the work to be carried out on your property.
▶ Planning permission – this concerns the quality of your design and how it relates to your building and the environment.

Building Regulations These are overseen by a Building Control Officer who operates from your local authority. The best way to contact the department is by telephoning your local council. Ask to speak to a representative at the Building Control office. Building Regulations primarily oversee the safety of your building works but also its efficiency. They are as follows:

▶ The structural integrity of your building
▶ Fire safety and resistance
▶ Resistance to moisture and damp
▶ The avoidance of toxic substances
▶ Sound insulation of your home
▶ Adequate ventilation
▶ Levels of hygiene
▶ Drainage and waste removal
▶ The efficiency and safety of your boiler
▶ Conservation of energy
▶ Safety in glazing matters

If any of the work that you are planning to undertake concerns these issues, you must contact a Building Control Officer. It's a good idea to have an initial discussion with them so they can outline the issues you will face. You will then need to complete a form detailing the work, which will be processed and commented on. This can take some time so it is essential that you complete this submission at the early stages of the project.

Your Building Control Officer will make regular visits during the course of the project to inspect the quality and safety of the work being carried out. When the project has been completed, the Building Control Officer will make a final inspection and issue a certificate demonstrating that the work complies with the Building Regulations and legal requirements. When selling your property you will need this certificate to prove that the work has been carried out safely and legitimately. You will also need it for household insurance so you must follow the guidelines and advice of your Building Control Officer.

Due to the complexity of the drawings that will be required, it can be advisable to get a builder or an architect to deal with the Building Control submission. They may additionally require the services of other professionals such as a structural engineer to produce drawings that satisfy structural calculations for the project.

Failure to contact your Building Control office can result in defective work having to be removed and reinstated to the legal requirements. Any non-compliance with this can result in legal action being taken.

Planning permission Planning permission will be needed if you intend to carry out any external works to your property. This can include:

► An extension
► Alterations to the façade such as new doors or windows
► Alterations to a listed building or one in a conservation area
► The addition of structures such as tall fences and out houses.
► A change in use of a property (i.e. from a warehouse to a loft-style home)
► The felling of certain trees situated within the boundaries of your property

In effect, any work that will alter the external appearance of your home or the environment around it will require you to contact your planning authority.

Associated with your local planning office is the authority that deals with properties in conservation areas and listed buildings. Although only certain projects that affect the external appearance of a building will need planning permission, any changes whatsoever to a listed building or one in a conservation area need special permission.

It's well worth going to talk to a representative of the planning authority prior to carrying out any work on your property. They will be able to inform you of any restrictions that exist on the property, such as conservation orders or rights of way. This can save you a lot of wasted time and money at the early stages of the project as they will outline what can and cannot be done to the property.

Following this, you can get a form to apply for planning permission from your council. You may then apply for outline planning permission, which is recommended. This will give you a general sense of whether you can go ahead officially but be careful, it does not mean that full planning permission has been granted. This will only be achieved with a series of drawings, including site plans, building plans and elevational drawings of the property to show its existing state and the proposed changes you wish to make. You may even be requested to supply samples of the materials that you intend to use. Unless you have the skills to carry out an accurate set of drawings, it makes sense to involve an architect at this stage of the project to fulfil the necessary requirements and to then apply for planning permission.

Planning permission can take up to six weeks to be considered. At this stage, the department may come back to you with requests for more information or for alterations to happen before you can start work. This can really slow up the construction process so it is essential that you look into your planning requirements well in advance of your intended start date. Work started without planning permission could mean you either have to apply for retrospective permission or are even instructed by your Planning Officer to take down the work – an expensive and painful process to be avoided at all costs.

Employing contractors

It is almost inevitable that at some stage of the process of redesigning your home you will need to employ the services of a builder, plumber or electrician. This can be a lengthy and costly process during which it is easy to encounter a number of pitfalls. Being cautious at this stage as to who you employ is a good idea in order to achieve a better result. With any of these trades, the best recommendation is by word of mouth from someone you trust. The chances are that if the contractor carried out good work for an acquaintance of yours, they will do equally good work for you.

Builders If you have had no personal recommendations of a local builder, try contacting the Confederation of Master Builders, which will recommend reputable and professional builders who may be interested in carrying out your work. Once you have decided on the project you wish to undertake, find at least three builders to tender (offer cost quotes) on your project. You need to know that the builder you end up employing is reputable, reliable and will carry out a high quality of work for you, so make some basic checks:

▶ Check the builder's financial records at Companies House as their bankruptcy could prove expensive if it occurs during the completion of your work.

▶ Check that the builder's insurance documentation covers the work they are to undertake in case a mistake occurs with the project or an accident happens to somebody while they are on-site.

▶ Ask the builder if you can inspect three of their completed projects to see the quality of the final scheme. If possible, speak to past clients of theirs to check they were happy with the service and quality provided by the builder. If the builder refuses this, you should walk away as they may be trying to hide a poor quality of service and work.

▶ You should also ask if they intend to bring in sub-contractors to carry out work that the builder is unable to complete, such as structural elements, the electrical wiring and plumbing. You need to make sure that if the builder does bring in sub-contractors he is responsible for the quality and efficiency of their work. You will have had no prior dealings with them so it would be very difficult for you to make a professional assessment on these points.

It is worth contacting builders several months before you intend to start work as many of the better ones will be booked up for some time in advance. Having to wait for a builder to be free to commence your project can really slow up the schedule for your completion date.

Writing a specification It's essential when you contact a builder that you know exactly what you are after. You must write down this information so that the builder can fully understand exactly what you want in terms of materials, the quality of the work and the time issues involved in the project. This information will form your specification document (see 'Implementing your design', pages 22–23).

You can use this document as part of the

process of approaching several builders so that they are clear as to what you want and can use it to cost the project. This costing exercise is known as the tender process and you should get at least three quotes for the same work as they can vary enormously.

Your specification document should be as detailed as possible, listing sizes, quantities, quality of finish, as well as materials, fixtures and fittings that you wish to be included in the scheme. Write this out neatly and clearly or create a detailed table on your computer. It will allow you to minimize any grey areas within the project but if you have any issues that you are unsure about, point this out to the builder and allow them to put down a figure that will cover possible costs associated with this. Providing a clear and detailed specification at the start of your project will let your builder know that you've thought clearly about what you want. Without it, costs can vary and rise dramatically. Builders may also bully you into using products that they can get discounts on and then charge you full price in an effort to top up their fees.

Within your specification, you should give an intended start and completion date, but you should not give an idea of your overall budget, except for items that you know the cost of, such as fixtures and fittings. It's also worth including a contingency fee of approximately 10 per cent of the cost of the overall scheme because inevitably as you start work, changes will occur due to unforeseen circumstances. This fee should be used only in an emergency and not for luxury items. It's essential that you get a firm idea of the costs of your project before you start work so that this can be agreed upon in the contract that you sign with your builder.

You need to discuss your method of payment with your builder and agree to split this over the course of the work that he carries out for you. Make it clear from the beginning that you intend to retain some of this payment – normally 5–10 per cent of the total fee – until the completion of the project to ensure that the builder will come back to finish any final alterations once the building work has had a chance to settle. If, due to unforeseen circumstances, additional work is necessary, you must get costs for this work before the builder starts on it as it is very difficult to discuss these once the work is completed.

A good working relationship with your builder is important but it's a good idea to use some form of contract with your builder as a safeguard in the event that you are unhappy with their work. In the UK, you can contact the Royal Institute of British Architects for a simple contract that outlines all of the possible basic scenarios and how they may be dealt with. It is important that you operate professionally with your builder and using a recognized form of contract with them is a key part of the management of your scheme. You should inspect the work of your builder regularly, but not constantly in a way that may hold up their progress. You should discuss any issues you have with the builder and keep notes of your conversations. With so many decisions that may need to be made, it's essential that you know what was said, by whom and on what date.

Unreliable trades people As with contractors (builders) you should check on your trades people (plumbers, electricians, plasterers, etc) and ask to inspect other jobs that they have undertaken. It's also a good idea to speak to their past clients to check on their reliability as a frequent trick that specialist trades people will play is to take on your job and then several others at the same time, throwing your schedule, and possibly your entire project, into chaos. This can be enormously frustrating, particularly when you need their work to co-ordinate with that of the other trades in order to complete the various stages of work in a room such as your bathroom or kitchen. If an unreliable trades person hasn't completed the necessary work, the others may have to down tools and charge you for their time, without being able to complete their part of the work.

My advice is that as soon as you have a suspicion that a trades person is unreliable, give them an official warning, then terminate your contract if the warning is not heeded as your project will only get further behind schedule, and costs (and stress levels!) can spiral if they continue to be unreliable. Whilst this can be a difficult thing to do, you do need to be very clear about how reliable you need your trades people to be, as it will only cost you money and stress if they are not compliant with your needs and schedules. It can be a good idea to write into your contract with that trades person a "frustration clause" that allows you to cancel your agreement and recover up front costs if work is not completed as agreed.

While this advice may seem negative, it's better to be safe than sorry.

Plumbers These are notoriously difficult people to deal with so finding a good, reliable and efficient plumber is necessary to cut down on your level of management and frustration. The best way to find a good plumber is again by personal recommendation. Ask friends, relatives and colleagues – inevitably somebody at some point will have used a plumber they can recommend.

When you meet one, check whether they are registered. In the UK this will be with one of two groups. CORGI-registered (Confederation of Registered Gas Installers) plumbers are qualified in gas installation so are competent at fitting gas boilers and heating appliances. Although this is not essential for all works to be carried out, it is necessary for safety certificates on items such as boilers and ventilation. Plumbers registered with the Institute of Plumbers (www.plumbers.org.uk) will have passed examinations or had extensive experience.

Again, you should write a specification of what you want your plumber to complete for you. This should include start and finish dates, the type of fittings you wish them to fit and the quality of finish you want. For example, do you want pipes in your bathroom to be surface-mounted and boxed-in or chased into the plasterwork and then re-covered?

Ask for a written quote so you will know what the final cost should be. This will change only if unforeseen costs arise. Ask your plumber how many men will be working on the job and how long the job will take and get them to write this down on the quote. You should also discuss the payment details, allowing for an initial, a mid and a final payment of 10 per cent – to be made only when the completed work is finished and has been allowed to run for a period of time to ensure there are no defects. Estimates on the cost of your work will vary dramatically so get quotes from at least three plumbers for the same work before you decide on the one to employ.

Get a cost breakdown on the work on its completion, so that you know where your money has gone. If any parts have been purchased on your behalf, ask to see the receipts.

Electricians Finding a good, reliable and efficient electrician is also key to the success and smooth running of your project. As before, ask friends and colleagues whether they can recommend someone. As with plumbers, an electrician may have to coordinate with various other trades (plumbers, builders and plasterers) at specific points during your project, making their schedule of work quite complicated in order for the project to run smoothly. This can be broken down into what is called 'first fixings' (the positioning of cables and socket boxes) and 'second fixings' (fitting the final socket covers and lighting fixtures).

When employing your electrician, you will need to provide a specification of what you want and where you want it. This specification should include your lighting outlets, how these will be operated (switches, dimmers or pulls) and the location of electric sockets and spurs (special sockets for fixed items such as cookers). It is worthwhile overspecifying the number of sockets you may need at this stage as fitting more of them later on will be much more costly.

As with the other trades, you should discuss payments including the initial, mid and final payment when the work is finished and you have tested the electrical system that has been fitted. Again, you should get three estimates which will include start and completion dates as times and costs will vary dramatically. You should also talk to past customers to discuss the electrician's reliability and efficiency.

Check that your electrician is registered with a body that assesses the technical capabilities of all its members and inspects samples of their work. In the UK this will be the National Inspection for Electrical Installation (www.niceic.org.uk).

It is now clear to most people that the environmental issue is no longer just the reserve of bearded hippies. The way we currently live is not one that we can globally sustain, partly because of climate change and partly due to reducing natural resources. When I talk about the environment, I am talking as much about the quality of the environment in your home as that outside it.

It is important to get a sense of scale when thinking about environmental issues. The room you are decorating is one of several in your house, a house that is one of several in your street, which exists as one of hundreds in your town or city; which is one of hundreds in your country, which in turn is one of hundreds of countries globally. For all of us, acting in an environmentally responsible manner starts at home, and should operate throughout the scale of local authorities, regional councils and national governments. It is everyone's responsibility to do their bit. It is that simple.

And the best thing of all is that it is really not that difficult. With a little thought and a little effort, we can all feel good about ourselves and our green conscience.

Greener homes

Green decision-making

Firstly, it should be said that acting in an eco-friendly way in our homes is all about finding a balance that suits you. Everything we do involves consumption and all consumption has an environmental impact, but the main thing is to limit it as much as possible. If you remember only one point, think about the green issues at stake when making decisions about your home and how you live in it.

An additional benefit is that many of the issues discussed on the following pages will actually save you money, either immediately or in the long run, so consider 'thinking green' as an investment in more ways than one. Some new technology – for example, solar panels, are still expensive for many people, but can be a worthwhile investment that will pay for itself in the long run, if you can afford it. If you can't, there is a wide range of things you can do that are really easy and cheap to do – even more so if you incorporate them into the early stages of moving into a new home.

The green ideas discussed below are encompassed by three headings – reduce, reuse and recycle:

▶ 'Reduce' is about cutting down the amount of energy and resources that we use, and covers everything from electricity, water and gas to wood, paper and metal.
▶ 'Reuse' is about finding new ways to use existing items – for example, re-covering an old sofa, using reclaimed timber bricks or even salvaged radiators.
▶ 'Recycle' is, of course, about how we recycle the products that pass through our homes and encompasses everything from kitchen waste to furniture.

Reducing is better than reusing, which is better than recycling in terms of energy use and resources. So how can we use the three Rs in our homes?

Reduce In many industries the idea of reducing energy use is implemented as a matter of course. For instance, new houses now have to comply with much lower energy-use standards, resulting in better insulated walls and windows, and energy-efficient boilers. But we can still do a lot more in other ways.

In the UK, for example, one-quarter of all carbon emissions comes from the energy used in heating and lighting our homes – either directly from them or from the power stations supplying them. By defining where energy is used inefficiently we can reduce the impact on global warming by reducing green house gases and saving money. Although we can't all rebuild our homes with better insulation, there are a number of energy- (and money-!) reducing options to think about. The following list shows ways of reducing energy and living more greenly:

Electricity

▶ When your old tungsten bulbs die (which they will after only 1,000 hours!), fit the light with either a lower wattage bulb or even better an energy-saving bulb. These last 12 times longer than standard bulbs and, although more expensive, will actually pay for themselves after six months of normal usage.

- Make the most of any available natural light by keeping your windows clean and unobstructed.
- Don't leave equipment like the television and video player on standby as they will continue to use electricity, thereby costing you money.
- When you buy new household appliances like a washing machine, tumble dryer or dishwasher, ask whether there are low-energy usage models available. The new energy-efficient fridges use 40 per cent less energy than old ones, but don't stand one next to a heat source.
- Use centrally heated radiators that are operated from your boiler rather than electrical radiators since electrical heating is dramatically less efficient and more costly.
- Fit non-essential lights like those in hallways or communal corridors with a timer button to reduce the amount of time they are left on.
- Don't overfill the kettle as unused hot water is a waste of electricity.
- Air-dry your wet clothes instead of using a dryer.

Water

- When you buy a new appliance make sure it is a low water usage model – particularly washing machines and dishwashers.
- Wash only full loads in your washing machine or dishwasher.
- Leaving a tap running while you brush your teeth uses up to 10 litres (2.6 gallons) of water a minute, so turn it on only when you need water.

- Use a bowl in your sink when washing up or washing vegetables – ten minutes of washing under running water can waste a staggering 100 litres (26 gallons) of water.
- Don't leave taps running unnecessarily and fix leaky taps with new washers – it's money down the drain and all that!
- Buy a dual-flush toilet cistern so you can reduce the amount of water you flush every time. Alternatively, fit a half-brick sealed in plastic into your cistern to reduce the amount of water used. Old cisterns use up to 9 litres (2–3 gallons) of water per flush while new ones use only 3 litres (0.7 gallons).
- Minimize when and how you water the garden.
- Install a shower. Showers use two-fifths of the water that a bath might, although a power shower will use the same amount as a bath so think before you buy one. Better than that, share a bath. Theoretically it uses only half the water... but is twice the fun!

Gas

- Get an energy-efficient boiler and save up to 32 per cent on your gas bill.
- Install a temperature control system for your heating – thermostats in your house, or better still, on each radiator, or even a time control switch so you can turn your boiler on and off when you need it.
- Turn down the temperature of your hot water – if it's scalding and you have to mix it with cold water then it's too hot and will be costing you money.
- Make sure your water storage tank is properly insulated.

▶ Insulate your roof to stop heat loss.

▶ Fit reflective panels behind radiators to kick the heat forwards. These can be as simple as wooden boards with silver foil glued to them and are amazingly effective.

▶ Fit shelves over your radiators to force the rising heat forwards into the room rather than towards the ceiling.

▶ Fit curtains that cover the window and drop only to the windowsill to stop heat rising up and out through the window.

▶ Cut down on unnecessary draughts beneath doors and through windows, which chill your home. Use foam strips around the window, key hole covers for doors and nylon brush draught excluders.

▶ Fit double glazing where your budget allows. This will reduce noise pollution and prevent heat loss. Choose it carefully as not only can cheap uPVC double glazing make an unsightly addition to your house but PVC is environmentally harmful – organizations like Greenpeace have a list of alternatives. If you can't afford double glazing, you can fit a purpose-made plastic sheeting known as renewable film over your windows during the winter months to retain warmth. Stick it all around the window frame then heat it with a hairdryer until it shrinks and tightens across the window. This will prevent you from opening the windows, and will need to be carefully removed when the weather turns warmer.

▶ Use the correct size of pans on your hob as energy is wasted if the heat misses the base of the pan. Also, by putting on the lids you can reduce the amount of energy required to keep your food cooking.

Other ways

▶ Buy only durable or repairable products. such as recyclable printer cartidges.

▶ Don't accept excess packaging and refuse plastic bags when you don't need them.

▶ Buy fresh fruit and vegetables rather than ready-packaged meals.

▶ Buy a bicycle and cut down on car journeys.

▶ Reduce the pollutants you put out into the environment via the drain by using eco-friendly washing-up liquids, detergents and washing powders.

▶ If you have small children, find out about local towelling nappy cleaning services, as disposables are very wasteful and damaging, with each one taking longer than an entire lifetime to decompose (96 years!) if put into a landfill rubbish site.

▶ Check out the website of your energy supplier or contact your local authority as there are a number of schemes and grants available to help you save – from cheap, energy-efficient lightbulbs and composters to grants for insulating your home and installing a more efficient boiler.

Reuse

▶ Buy your electrical energy from a green supplier. You could very easily switch to electricity from renewable sources like wind and solar power.

▶ Buy wood from a reputable source – many suppliers now only sell wood bought from well-managed sustainable forests. This is regulated in by the FSC (Forest Stewardship Council) and any timber should have its stamp of approval – if it doesn't, ask your retailer.

► Fit photo-voltaic cells or solar heating panels to your roof. They won't fulfil your entire energy needs but will significantly cut down on your bills, and pay for themselves in time. In the UK, you can contact the Centre for Alternative Technology for the most up-to-date information and the possibility of grants to help fund their installation.

► Make sure that the products you buy come from suppliers with the same level of environmental beliefs and commitments as you. The best way to do this in the UK is to contact the Ethical Consumer Research Association, a great resource full of information on all types of products and services, to help you put your money where your mouth is!

► Buy rechargeable batteries, or use wind-up radios and torches. You can also recycle your car battery when it dies – contact your local council.

► Use the organic waste from your kitchen as a fertilizer by making your own compost, instead of buying peat-based commercial compost. Peat is a valuable natural resource that takes thousands of years to produce.

Recycle Many countries now run doorstep recycling schemes where separated waste products are collected by a single vehicle. If this is not the case where you live, it still makes sense to recycle but store up any products you may have and take them to recycling banks in one go.

There is now a massive range of products made from recycled materials and it is fast becoming the most exciting area of design as designers are coming up with ever more ingenious ways of utilizing what was once regarded as waste but now seen as a valuable resource. It really will be the design revolution of our age, so join in and give them something to work with.

► Find a place at home to store glass, paper, plastics and cans (steel and aluminium) ready for the recycling banks or buy a multi-compartment bin to fit in your kitchen.

► Instead of buying a new piece of furniture, use your imagination and find a way of giving an old piece a new lease of life – for example, recover a chair or paint it.

► If you do want to get rid of an appliance like an old computer, electrical item or a usable piece of furniture research the internet or phone your council, as there are now a growing number of local schemes that will fix and restore items to sell them on for charitable purposes, or give them to worthy causes.

► Be ingenious. If you can find a way of reusing an item it will save you money and maybe even give you pleasure. There are a number of items that can be reused within the home – for example, glass jars reused as storage jars.

► Keep old plastic bags and reuse them when shopping – we really don't need as many as we are given. Even better is to use an alternative like a canvas or string bag instead, then nothing is wasted.

Quality of life As well as the three Rs that will help our homes to be environmentally conscious it is essential to remember the quality of our own environments. The synthetic products with which we fill our homes and live with every day can be detrimental to the quality of the air and living conditions. Added to the fact that our homes now have less natural ventilation than they used to, this means that it is easy for toxins to build up, which can lead to an increase in allergies and a general decrease in health. Watch out for the following elements:

▶ The products of the combustion of materials such as coal, tobacco, gas, candles and even joss sticks – many of these produce gases such as carbon monoxide, which need adequate ventilation to prevent them from building up.

▶ The vapours and gases that build up from household products such as solvents, glues and paints – the general rule is that if it smells unpleasant and makes you recoil, then it probably is and you don't want it in your house. The slow release of vapours from products, known as 'off-gassing', comes from a variety of materials:

Paints – buy paints with a low level of volatile organic compounds (VOCs). VOCs are nasty heavy toxins, which can be ingested even by mouth as they release gas and drop from the paint on the walls to the floor. They are found largely in oil-based gloss and eggshell paints. You really don't want these in your bedroom, so try organic paints, natural finishes such as beeswax, and natural cleaners like borax, ammonia and vinegar for sweet dreams! For a list of suppliers search the internet under 'organic paints'.

Resins and varnishes (used on floors and furniture)

Polyurethane and polystyrene (used for insulation and some furniture such as beanbags).

Synthetic textiles in furniture, curtains and especially carpets – try to buy only carpets with a natural backing such as hessian, or use natural fibre carpets such as jute and coir. Reducing the number of carpets you have will lower the build-up of dust in your home.

▶ Formaldehyde – one of the chemicals known to contribute to 'Sick Building Syndrome', formaldehyde is used in the glue that bonds together many types of particle board, such as chipboard and MDF (medium-density fibreboard). Particle board is now more common than ever as it forms the backing to many types of laminate flooring. Its convenience and cheap cost is appealing but try to reduce the amount you use, particularly in areas such as bedrooms, where you spend prolonged periods of time. Try using natural materials such as cork, linoleum or wooden boards instead.

▶ Airborne fibres such as those caused by materials like asbestos – if you can't identify a particular material, or suspect that it might be asbestos then consult an expert. Asbestos in sheet form is a hard board with a clay- or stone-like feel to it and a fibrous surface texture. It was fitted during the 1950s and 1960s but has since been banned. All asbestos must be removed by professionals, as disturbing it will release carcinogenic particles into the air, and so requires proper safety equipment and a licence to move and dispose of it.

▶ Water born pollutants – check the quality of your tap water and whether it is brought to you in old-style lead pipes. If it is, contact your local water supplier about getting these removed. It may also be worth installing a water filter.

▶ Older paints – those dating back to the 1970s may have a high lead content and should be carefully stripped back whilst wearing a dust mask and gloves and repainted.

▶ Dust – the build-up of dust in furnishings and carpeting encourages dust mites, which can lead to allergies. Prevent it building up by vacuuming regularly or by cutting down on the number of dust-trapping materials in your home such as fabrics and wall-to-wall carpets.

Greener spaces checklist

▶ Kitchen/utility room/dining room

Make a space to store plastics, cans, paper and glass for recycling

Reuse plastic carrier bags

Buy only energy- and water-saving appliances

Don't leave taps running

Fit a water filter for drinking and washing

Compost kitchen waste if you have a garden

Think about the room's ventilation

Don't boil more water than necessary in your kettle

Use small pots and pans

Operate dishwashers, washing machines and tumble dryers at full-load capacity

▶ Bathroom

Don't leave taps running

Consider water-saving features – for example, a dual-flush toilet cistern, showers versus baths

Insulate your water tank

Ensure you have good ventilation

Consider central heating rather than electric towel rails

Choose linoleum or cork flooring rather than PVC

▶ Bedrooms

Avoid excessive toxins – for example, in flooring materials

Ensure you have good ventilation

Prevent build-up of dust

Use energy-saving lightbulbs

Don't leave a television on stand-by mode

Fit shelving over radiators

Use low-VOC paint

▶ Lounge

Don't leave electrical equipment on stand-by mode

Use different levels of lighting and energy-saving lightbulbs

Fit shelving over radiators

▶ Corridors

Fit lights with energy-saving lightbulbs and a timer button

Avoid wall-to-wall carpeting

▶ External space

Air-dry wet clothes

Minimize watering the garden

Useful green websites

Although the majority of these websites are UK based, much of the information they provide is still relevant to those living in other countries. You will also find that almost every country has similar organisations.

The Association for Environment Conscious Building
Excellent information and an extensive list of approved suppliers
Website: www.aecb.net

Centre for Alternative Technology
Lots of advice on sustainable living (e.g. photovoltaic cells and solar heating information) and organic gardening
Website: www.cat.org.uk

The Construction Resource Centre
All sorts of information, including green building products
Website: www.ecoconstruct.com

The Ethical Consumer Research Association
An amazing resource into ethical buying power. The group will tell you who is good to buy from and who isn't – covering everything from washing powder and batteries to bricks and mortgages
Website: www.ethicalconsumer.org

Industry Council for Electronic Equipment Recycling (ICER)
A list of commercial recyclers of fridges, washing machines etc.
Website: www.icer.org.uk

Friends of the Earth
A great information service that can answer all sorts of questions
Website: www.foei.org

Forest Stewardship Council (FSC)
A database of products made from well-managed and sustainable forests
Website: www.fsc-uk.info

Reuze
Information on how to recycle a huge variety of items, such as furniture, electrical appliances, carpets, pots and pans etc. Also provides the Furniture Recycling Network directory which has a list of organisations that will reuse and redistribute old furniture.
Website: www.reuze.co.uk/recycle

Recycle More
Information on how to increase recycling rates in your home, school or business
Website: www.recycle-more.co.uk

Waste Connect
A database of all recycling facilities in the UK
Website: www.wastepoint.co.uk

Having the right tools for the job in hand really makes a massive difference when you're undertaking do-it-yourself projects. It will make jobs quicker and easier to accomplish, allowing you to complete them painlessly and professionally. Without them, you could turn a simple task into an expensive emergency, eventually requiring a professional to come in and clean up the mess!

Getting together a basic tool box with the right tools need not be expensive, and I guarantee you will appreciate it when it's most needed. You can visit your local hardware store, a major do-it-yourself centre or even a local market, where there will often be a stall selling a range of tools at great prices.

Opposite are listed a basic range of tools that are worth collecting for your tool box, which should enable you to carry out a range of different jobs around the home.

Tool box and glossary

General

Alun keys – hexagonal keys for assembling flat-packed furniture

Automatic wire strippers – quick and easy to use, these make changing a plug a joy!

Bench saw – for general cutting.

Bradawl – pointed screwdriver for making small holes in wood or other soft materials for positioning screws.

Claw hammer – buy a medium one for general purpose and removing nails.

Clip-on vice – clips onto a worksurface or table to hold materials you are working on.

Craft knife – for detailed cutting of, for example, stencils. The blades blunt quickly so buy one with replaceable blades or one where you can snap off the old ones easily.

Craft knife, heavy duty – for cutting a variety of thicker materials such as carpet. Buy one with a retractable blade (which is replaceable) and a good grip.

Drill and drill bits – buy a cordless (at least 12-volt), rechargeable, battery-operated drill for ease and practicality, but an electric drill for greater power. Purchase a range of drill bits in different sizes for drilling into masonry, wood and metals or plastics. In addition, buy a wire brush attachment for sanding down objects or removing paint.

Hacksaw – this has a metal tubular frame and a fine tooth blade, and is used for cutting metal and plastic.

Metal straight edge/ruler – essential for cutting against with a craft knife.

Mole wrench – pliers with a lockable jaw, which makes them great for gripping objects or to use as a mini-clamp.

Multi-section tool box – with room for tools and fittings like nails and screws. It allows you to see what tools are where and should be easy to carry and store.

Pencils – for easily removed marking out lines

Pliers, pincer-nosed – the smaller nose and jaws makes pulling nails out of floors much more easily done.

Pliers, slip joint – with an adjustable head for larger nuts and bolts.

Pliers, snub-nosed – good for cutting wire and general gripping. Buy ones with easy-to-hold rubber handles.

Plumb line – basically a string and a weight with a point on it, it allows you to put a vertical line on a wall or project a point on the ceiling on to the floor.

Retractable steel tape measure – buy a 3 or 5 metre (10 or 16 ft) metal tape measure with a lock to stop the tape retracting.

Scissors – for all sorts of do-it-yourself and craft tasks.

Screwdriver, cross-head – for cross-head screws. Buy a medium and small size; again, make sure the handle is comfortable and easy to grip.

Screwdriver, flat-head – buy a small, medium and large size for general and electrical use. Make sure the handle offers a good comfortable grip.

Spirit level – a small 30 cm (12 in) long spirit level is essential when hanging pictures or fitting shelves to walls to check the horizontal and vertical alignment.

Safety

Dust mask – required to reduce the dangerous intake of dust or fibre particles. Also provides some protection from flying particles, like those produced by drilling.

Extension lead – a 10 m (33 ft) lead will allow you to work safely without stretching cables.

Gloves – choose fabric or leather – a must for any dangerous task.

RCD (residual current device) – acts as a circuit breaker to prevent electrocution if a wire gets cut or damaged. Should be used with any power tool or extension lead.

Safety goggles – essential to protect your eyes from particles of dust, dirt or dangerous liquids.

Adhesives and fittings

Electrical tape – good for insulating electrical cables and tying back cables.

Glue – buy super and general purpose glue.

Hooks – buy a range of sizes for a variety of tasks.

Invisible thread – for hanging objects 'magically' from the ceiling.

Multi-purpose spray-on oil – for dealing with squeaky doors, stiff locks and a variety of other household jobs.

Nails, masonry – for knocking directly into masonry walls.

Nails, wood – get different sizes for a variety of jobs.

Plasterboard wall plugs – for putting screws in plasterboard walls, but don't overload them as they don't have the strength of those in a masonry wall.

Plastic cable ties – great for tidying cables and other jobs. Buy a variety of sizes.

Rawl plugs – for putting screws in masonry walls. Buy a range of sizes.

Screws – have a range of sizes and widths to carry out a variety of different jobs.

Self-adhesive wall cable tidies – easier than the cable tidies you have to bash into the wall with a hammer.

Staple gun – quick and easy to use for upholstery needs.

Thin wire – great for all sorts of craft jobs.

Decorating

Dust sheets – use old sheets or curtains, or buy cotton sheets that you can reuse. Stick them to the floor for safety using masking tape.

Filling knife – for repairing holes in walls with filler.

Masking tape – buy high-tack tape for sticking items such as dust sheets to the floor and special low-tack tape for masking off walls without pulling off paint.

Paint brushes – buy a range of different sizes for floors, walls, details and woodwork.

Paint kettle – for decanting the paint into. It is easier to hold than a paint can while up a ladder.

Rollers – buy a big one (30 cm/12 in long) for general use and a small one (10 cm/4 in long) for areas such as behind radiators.

Sanding block – a foam block with a rough textured finish. The easiest way of sanding down plaster wall filler.

Scraper – for removing wallpaper and cleaning up walls.

Wire brush – for cleaning walls.

Glossary

Airbrick A perforated wall brick that allows movement of air from the inside out and vice versa. Must be left unobstructed to prevent the build-up of condensation and gas.

Architrave The profiled or decorative wooden moulding around a door or window.

Balustrade The vertical barrier topped by a hand rail, which acts as a safety barrier along a staircase. Also known as banisters.

Base coat The first layer of paint on a surface, which ensures the top decorative coat goes on smoothly and evenly.

Carcass The base of the units in your kitchen that doors fix to and your work surface sits on.

Cavity wall A wall comprising two solid vertical surfaces (board or masonry) with a fixed gap in between, which can be used for insulation.

Chasing Cutting a channel into a wall or solid floor surface to allow pipes or cables to be concealed within, before being covered over to match the existing surface and finish.

Chipboard A flat board made from small chips of wood glued together. Often used as a base for flooring or in kitchens as the base for worksurfaces and doors. It swells and reacts badly to water.

Cornice A decorative moulding made of plaster or polystyrene that covers the join between walls and ceiling.

Countersunk A means of recessing a screw head so that it sits flush with the surface it is fixed into.

Dado rail A wooden rail fixed to the wall (normally about waist height), originally intended to protect walls from damaging wear from the backs of chairs. Now used primarily as a decorative feature to give a room an altered sense of proportion.

Damp-proof membrane Known as a DPM, a water-impervious sheet situated below the ground floor or basement of a property, intended to prevent damp from rising up into the property. Similar to a damp-proof course.

Drain An open gulley or the main sewage outlet point for the house, located nearby with an inspection pit and solid removable cover.

Eaves The part of the roof that projects beyond the walls.

Escutcheon (plate) A decorative cover for the keyhole of an exterior door, preventing draughts.

Extension Any additional room or space added to the original floor plan of a property.

Fascia A panel that covers unsightly details.

Finial A usually decorative end cap to a curtain pole.

Fuse box The electrical safety unit that connects the mains electricity supply to that of your home. It allows you to turn off the electricity supply (thereby preventing electrocution) when work needs to be carried out on any part of the electrical system, and will shut down the supply if a fault occurs. Make sure you know its location.

Galvanized A mottled greyish protective layer used to cover steel to prevent it from rusting.

Glaze A protective coat that can be applied to a surface for decorative effect (e.g. a crackle glaze) or added to a material during production (e.g. wall tiles).

Grain The markings on wood which gives it a visual sense of direction. When sanding wood, always work in the direction of the grain for a smooth finish.

Gulley A channel used for directing the flow of water, often from a roof or related to a drainage detail.

Gutter A channel for directing rainwater flowing off the roof of a property into the drainage system. Damaged gutters can cause damp on the interior of a property.

Hardwood The timber from a deciduous tree. Generally stronger and longer lasting than a softwood and therefore more expensive.

Insulation A material that prevents the movement of heat or sound from your home. Insulation can be fitted to floors, walls, ceilings and in roof spaces.

Joist A horizontal structural beam made of wood, steel or concrete, which is used to support the weight of the floor or roof above it.

Key A term used to describe abrasions made on a surface (often by sandpaper) in order to allow a finish such as paint or varnish to adhere well to it.

Kicking plate A low-level protective strip fixed to a door or the bottom of kitchen units to prevent damage to the surface beneath it from knock and scratches.

Lead The material used in roofs to prevent water from entering the property – it can be easily manipulated to mould around difficult shapes. If your roof leaks it may be due to defective lead work.

Lintel The structural beam that supports the fabric of a building above a door or window.

Mains A term used to define any of the utilities that enter your home, such as the water, electrical or gas mains. They will be met by a meter and a safety valve of some type in order to shut it off in case of an emergency.

Marbling A decorative paint effect used on a surface like wood to recreate the effect of marble. Often used to decorate the fronts of fireplaces.

Mastic A rubbery liquid used to seal the edges of surfaces that are likely to get wet, such as baths, basins, showers, sinks and work-surfaces. It is applied from a tube and worked into the joint to be sealed.

MDF (medium-density fibreboard) A solid wooden board that comes in a variety of thicknesses and is made of wood fibres glued together with a formaldehyde resin glue. Easily damaged by water unless sealed.

Mullion A vertical member of a window frame used to divide one pane of glass from another.

Nosing The rounded front edge of a stair tread.

Off-gas The slow release of (often toxic) gases into the surrounding environment.

Party wall The wall between you and your neighbour, over which you share ownership.

Plasterboard Solid board made of gypsum plaster covered on both sides with a tough lining paper that can then be decorated onto.

Primer A protective coat of paint used on woods and metals, in much the same way as a base coat, before the top coat is added.

Pile The fibres that raise out of the backing of a carpet, and which can be of varying lengths.

Purlin A horizontal beam of wood in the roof that supports angled sloping rafters above it.

Rafters The sloping timber beams in the roof that are part of the structural system.

Recessed When an object is mounted flush with the surface that it is fitted into, for example recessed lights in a ceiling, where the workings of the light are concealed in the ceiling cavity.

Render The layer of cement-based mortar that covers and protects external brickwork.

Riser The vertical part of a stair that rises from the tread.

Screed A thin layer of mortar applied to horizontal surfaces to give them a smooth finish.

Sill The horizontal surface at the bottom edge of a window or door.

Skirting board The wooden protective strip at the base of the wall which prevents damage from knocks and scrapes.

Softwood The timber from a coniferous tree, for example pine. Generally weaker and cheaper than hardwood.

Soil stack The large pipe that carries waste from the toilet to the drains and sewage system.

Spur A fixed (without a plug) electrical outlet for items such as radiators and cookers.

Subsidence The sinking of part of a building due to foundations built on soil that is unable to hold the weight of the building.

Surface mounted Any element that is fixed directly on to a surface, for example surface-mounted lights.

Threshold The dividing element between two areas. Generally used to define the step between an interior and exterior space.

Thermostat An electrical device used to control the temperature inside a house by turning on the heating through an on/off switch, which can be set to specific temperatures.

Top coat The final protective and decorative layer of a painted surface.

Trap A twisted section of pipe in a sink or toilet that contains water as a means of preventing the rise of bad-smelling gases.

Tread The horizontal plane of a step that you walk on.

Undercoat A layer of paint applied to primer and used to build up the protective layers of paint on a surface.

Underpinning The process carried out to reinforce the inadequate foundations of a building.

Warp The twist in a piece of wood created by heat or damp.

Waste pipe The pipe that carries away used water from a sink, basin or electrical water-using appliance like a washing machine.

Index

Page numbers in *italics* indicate separate illustrations.

Picture credits and acknowledgements:

Abode: Simon Whitmore 28a, 94; Tim Imrie 39, 45, 90c, 102, 113, 133, 135, 183, 186, 190, 197a, 212 ; James White 40, 217, 222; Trevor Richards 62a; Neil Davis 93, 202b, 207; Bernard O'Sullivan 105, 188, 220; Trevor Richards 143, 148, 225; Brett Prestidge 165d; Tony Hall 167

Abby Franklin: 211

Arcaid: David Churchill 28b, 49, 145, 159; Richard Powers 51a, 68b, 123, 125, 158, 161, 174, 195, 204, 208, 213; Richard Bryant 57, 139, 144b, 165a, 178, 208, 219; Martine Hamilton 89; Gary Hamil 100a, 112; Alan Weintraub 104, Premium 197b; Nicholas Kane 202a, 206

Oliver Heath: 14, 15, 16, 17a, 17b, 17c, 21, 48a, 72, 73, 74, 114, 154, 157, 166, 168, 193, 194a, 223

Red Cover: Chris Tubbs 26, 34, 103; Steve Dalton 27a; Tim Evan-Cook 29, 33; Homebase 32; Graham Atkins-Hughs 71, 117,182 ; Jake Fitzjones 87, 90a, 126, 155 ; Henry Wilson 90e; Winfried Heinze 97, 177; Ed Reeve 100b; James Mitchell 179; Huntley Hedworth 192

www.elizabethwhiting.com: David Giles 68d; Tom Leighton 79, 101, 116, 118; 203; Mark Luscombe-White 80, 90b, 136; Andreas von Einsiedel 90d; 'Neil Davis 121, 162a; Tim Street-Porter 141, Niall McDermot 165b; Rodney Hyett 165c; Di Lewis 180

The publishers would like to extend a special thanks to the following suppliers who have kindly lent pictures of their products:

Lighting:
Artemide (www.artemide.com, 020 7631 5200) 42a, 42b, 42c, 44a, 46b, 48b, 48c; Osram (www.osram.co.uk, e-mail: csc@osram.co.uk, 01744 812 221) 44b, 46a, 46c, 46d, 52a, 52b, 52c, 53a; Candles on the Web Ltd (www.candlesontheweb.co.uk, 020 8961 1621) 48d; Mathmos (www.mathmos.co.uk, 020 7549 2700) 51b; Schott Uk Ltd (www.schott.com, 01302 361574) 54b; Intalite UK (www.intalite.co.uk, e-mail: matt@ intalite.co.uk, 020 8543 6366) 54c ;

Blinds:
Eclectics Contemporary Blinds Collection (www.eclectics.co.uk, 0870 010 2211) 41a, 41b, 75, 98, 99a, 99b, 217

Wall finishes:
Dulux (www.dulux.co.uk, 01753 550555) 27b, 61, 173, 194b; Polycell (www.polycell.co.uk, 01753 550555 for stockist information) 58; Artex-Rawlplug Limited (www.artex-rawlplug.co.uk, 0115 984 9123) 59; Crown Paints (www.crownpaint.co.uk, 0870 240 1127) 60; The Stencil Library (www.stencil-library.com, 01661 844844) 62b; Cole & Son (Wallpapers) Ltd (www.cole-and-son.com, 020 8442 8844) 64a, 64e; Anaglypta® a division of CWV Group Ltd (www.anaglypta.co.uk, advice line: 01254 870838) 64b;

Muraspec Wall Coverings (www.muraspec.com, e-mail: customerservices@muraspec.com, 08705 117 118) 64c, 64d; Fired Earth Interiors: (www.firedearth.com, 01295 814300) 66a, 66b, 68c; Original Stone Direct (www.originalstoneco. co.uk, 0800 0832 2283) 66c

Flooring:
Puhos Board (UK) Limited (www.puhosboard.com, 01582 461717) 76; Siesta Cork Tile Company (www.siestacork tiles.co.uk, 020 8683 4055) 77a; Marmoleum, Forbo Flooring (www.marmoleum.co.uk, 0800 731 2369) 77b; Amtico (www.amtico. com, 0121 745 0868) p.78a; Dalsouple (www.dalsouple.com, 01278 727733) 78b; Fired Earth Interiors (www.firedearth.com, 01295 814300) 81a, 81b, 82a, 221; Brintons Ltd (www.brintons.net, 01562 820000) 82b; Crucial Trading (www.crucial-trading.com, 01562 743747) 83a, b, c, d; Heuga by Interface Europe Ltd (www.huegaathome.com, email: enquiries@eu.interfaceinc.com, 0800 085 7979) 85a; Dentro Spain SL (www.dentro.co.uk) 85b

Bathrooms:
Fired Earth Interiors (www.firedearth.com, 01295 814300) 144a, 147a, 147b

Kitchen work surfaces:
Corian® solid surface by DuPont (www.corian.co.uk, 0800 962116) 162b; Cast Advanced Concretes Ltd. (www.castadvancedconcretes. com, 01929 480757) 162c